Skyscrapers, Hemlines and the Eddie Murphy Rule

Skyscrapers, Hemlines and the Eddie Murphy Rule

Life's Hidden Laws, Rules and Theories

Philip Gooden

Bloomsbury Information
An imprint of Bloomsbury Publishing Plc

B L O O M S B U R Y
LONDON · NEW DELHI · NEW YORK · SYDNEY

Bloomsbury Information
An imprint of Bloomsbury Publishing Plc

50 Bedford Square	1385 Broadway
London	New York
WC1B 3DP	NY 10018
UK	USA

www.bloomsbury.com

BLOOMSBURY and the Diana logo are trademarks of Bloomsbury Publishing Plc

First published 2015

British Library Cataloguing-in-Publication Data
A catalogue record for this book is available from the British Library.

ISBN: HB: 978-1-4729-1502-3
ePDF: 978-1-4729-1504-7
ePub: 978-1-4729-1503-0

Library of Congress Cataloging-in-Publication Data
Gooden, Philip.
Skyscrapers, hemlines and the Eddie Murphy Rule : life's hidden laws,
rules and theories / Philip Gooden.
pages cm
ISBN 978-1-4729-1502-3 (hardback) - ISBN 978-1-4729-1503-0 (ebook) -
ISBN 978-1-4729-1504-7 (epdf) 1. Conduct of life. I. Title.
BJ1521.G63 2015
082 – dc23
2015004378

Typeset by Newgen Knowledge Works (P) Ltd., Chennai, India
Printed and bound in India

Contents

3 Arts 71

Introduction

There was a time when rules and laws and theories were the preserve of kings and parliamentarians, of scientists and religious leaders. True, away from their elevated viewpoint, there was always a brisk trade in proverbs and axioms of the 'stitch in time saves nine' variety, but these were rarely labelled as laws or given the status of theories. In fact, proverbs tend to be closer to folk-lore than to science, and for all their common-sense they often have a touch of superstition and are occasionally contradictory. (*Many hands make light work* but *Too many cooks spoil the broth*; *Look before you leap* even though *He who hesitates is lost*.)

It's impossible to give a precise date to the democratization of the informal law and the unwritten rule, or to pinpoint the moment when it became possible for anyone to come up with his or her own pithy observation which, provided it catches on, ensures a place for the discoverer in debate, in history and even in the dictionaries. Although, as it happens, the person who discovers a law and the person who names it may be two entirely different people (see Stigler's Law of Eponymy). The process of law-making really gets under way sometime in the middle of the twentieth century and starts to accelerate towards the close of the century. World War II saw the invention of two imaginary figures known as Chad and Kilroy – respectively, British and American – whose insubordination, evasiveness and wry commentary point towards the archetypal Murphy's Law, first noted in 1951. The promulgation of Parkinson's Law in 1955, appearing first without the name of Cyril Northcote Parkinson in an *Economist* article, ushered in a period of laws and rules relating to office life and work such as the Peter Principle or the Dilbert Principle.

More recently, it is no coincidence that the rise of the Internet and the online world, with its odd mixture of protocol and lawlessness, has seen the birth of many rules and principles. Such is the rate of growth here that what is a year old is already dated while to go ten years back is to enter another era. Of the more than 140 rules, laws and theories described and discussed in this book, the great majority date from the last fifty years.

How are laws established? They seem to be a product half of accident, half of design, in that their 'success' is largely out of the hands of their creator. Yes, as I just said, anyone can come up with the pithy rule or quasi-scientific observation, but it has to catch on. This catching-on is the crucial thing. As an example, take a 'law' which has emerged at the very moment I'm writing this, mid-January 2015. In a blog dated 10 January 2015 on his Unqualified Offerings site, Jim Henley decided to formulate Jim's Rule of Buts which states: 'In any charged conversation, find any statement containing the conjunction "but" and reverse the clauses.' As an example Henley offers, 'I'm sorry I yelled at you, but what you said made me really angry.' He points out that despite appearances the two halves of this semi-apology are not really equal since what follows the 'but' always dominates what comes before it. If you're the one saying these words and genuinely want to express regret then you ought to reverse their order. ('What you said made me really angry but I'm sorry I yelled at you.') Henley is right and it's an interesting point. Jim's Rule of Buts is an arresting title, too, more so in the United States perhaps where 'butt' is a familiar piece of slang. Will Jim's Rule of Buts catch on though, becoming enshrined as a 'proper' law? Maybe it will, though I suspect it's a little too refined, a bit too recherché, to become truly popular. But the point remains: we can all be our own lawmakers.

Perhaps a more significant question than how laws, rules and theories come to be established is why they should be needed in the first place. A large number, especially in politics and economics, are predictive and emerge out of our need to know what might happen in the future. For some this isn't just a matter of passing curiosity but of their livelihoods, which is one reason why there are so many laws and theories predicting electoral results or how shares and market prices are going to move. Others laws have an element of science and are the product of the research centre or the sociological department yet can still appeal to the non-specialist (in this book, e.g., Longfellow's Lift Rules or Planetary Naming Rules or the Law of Urination). Writers, as one would expect, are particularly fond of laying down the law, sometimes about the business of writing but also about the rules which govern genres like crime or science fiction. Then there is a whole tranche of what I have called 'grumpy old laws', essentially lamenting that things ain't what they used to be, a familiar idea but one often expressed with scornful precision (see Hutber's Law). And there are the many legal affiliates and descendants of Murphy and Sod, each expressing with fatalism, bitterness or irony that things in this world rarely work out as we expect them to.

Skyscrapers, Hemlines and the Eddie Murphy Rule is divided into sections covering areas such as politics, physical survival, rules in film and so on. There is a small section at the end dealing with actual laws. The book is a miscellany and not a life-style guide or 'how to succeed' manual. The only guiding principle is that the laws, rules, theories and principles contained in it should be curious or informative or amusing or, sometimes, all three of those things.

I would like to thank Alana Clogan and Rosie Bick at Bloomsbury for their advice and support in writing this book, and Neil Marsden and Ben Spicer for assistance in ransacking the remoter corners of the Internet and elsewhere for unusual laws and rules.

Philip Gooden
January 2015

1

Politics

There are two areas of life where the specialists and the insiders are always anxious to know what's going to happen in the future: politics and economics. The key question for both groups is the same. What do I have to do next in order to earn myself more votes/money? Hence the increasing reliance on focus groups and opinion polls in politics, and the rash of statistical analyses, charts, graphs, predictions and prognoses in the financial world. Even though it sometimes seems as if the price of failure for bankers and financiers is a bigger bonus, things are more serious for politicians who get it badly wrong since they may be out of a job at the next election. So the Politics section of this book begins with some predictive rules and laws for gazing into the future, before moving on to Foreign Affairs and Home Affairs.

Crystal balls

The Redskins Rule and the Slaphead Rule

Nobody can wait for the result of an election but everybody has to. In the United States in particular, this agonizing situation has led to a full-scale industry which employs thousands of pollsters, predictors and psephologists to consult the public with a frequency that becomes almost demented as a presidential election draws near. But there are less orthodox, albeit less scientific, methods of trying to work out who will walk into the White House. The most notable of these is the Redskins Rule.

The Washington Redskins[1] are an American team in the National Football League (NFL). Based in Virginia and representing the capital of the country, the team inadvertently gave birth to a rule which states that:

> If the Redskins win their last home game before the election, the party that won the previous election wins the next election and if the Redskins lose, the challenging party's candidate wins.

---

[1] For some years controversy has simmered around the Redskin name on the grounds that it is racially offensive to Native Americans. In 2013 President Obama weighed in, saying that the owner of the team should think about changing it. Alternative names include 'Chief' and 'Skins'. The owner, Daniel Snyder, may be reluctant to change, but the value of his sports franchise – $1.55 billion, according to Forbes magazine – rates it at number four in the world (Manchester United are first), and may prompt a change. In 2014 the team was deprived of its protection against copyright infringement by the US Patent Office, so opening it to potential losses of millions of dollars in merchandize through piracy.

Although applied retrospectively, the Redskins Rule was a fairly recent discovery/invention by an executive in a US sports statistics company. Steve Hirdt was looking for an election-related graphic for a TV sports show and found the pattern just before a Redskins' home game against the Tennessee Titans on 30 October 2000. The figures were double-checked and with remarkable consistency they showed that a win or loss for the Redskins had been an accurate pointer to a win or loss for the incumbent political party from 1940 onwards. The election of 7 November 2000 pitted Republican George W. Bush against Democrat Al Gore; a week previously the Redskins had lost to the Tennessee Titans, and therefore the incumbent party (the Democrats under Bill Clinton) duly lost their hold on the White House. Although the result was disputed because Gore won the popular vote (more people) while Bush won the electoral college votes (more states), the Redskins Rule held true. There was a glitch in 2004 when Bush again won against John Kerry even though the Redskins lost their home match that year which meant, according to the rule, that the incumbent's party should have lost. The ingenious Steve Hirdt rejigged the rule to take account of the popular vote/electoral college vote distinction.

In early November 2012 a single NFL match caused elation for the Republicans and gloom among the more superstitious Democrats when the Redskins lost (to the Carolina Panthers). According to the Redskins Rule, this meant that Barack Obama would not be reelected to the White House in what had been a bitterly contested contest, since his had been the incumbent party following the election of 2008. This time the Redskins Rule foreshadowed a victory for the Republican candidate, Mitt Romney. Yet in November 2012, it was Obama who won for a second time and with a clear majority. The Redskins Rule stumbled, and its creator graciously laid it to rest, declaring: 'I'm actually not too melancholy . . . To tell you the truth, I think the rule has run its course.'

There are several other unofficial methods of predicting the election outcome for the US presidency. Perhaps the most counter-intuitive is that, of the two – supposedly scary – halloween masks which feature the candidates, it is the one which sells better which signals the winner. So, in 2008 Obama's image comfortably outsold John McCain's as it did Mitt Romney's in 2012. An alternative method also combines profit with polling. Since 2000, the 7-Eleven chain have been selling their pre-election take-away coffee in blue (Democrat candidate) and red (Republican candidate) paper cups. This count-the-cups system has, so far, proved at least as reliable as any more scientific and expensive polling.

Election-winner rules which combine sense, intuition and craziness are not confined to the United States. The British political blogger and mischief-monger, Guido Fawkes (aka Paul Staines), lays down this law: 'The age old rule in British politics is that bald men do not beat rivals with a full head of hair. Think Tony Blair versus William Hague, Iain Duncan Smith and Michael Howard, nor can we forget Maggie versus Kinnock, in every election the slaphead loses.'

The Incumbent Rule

This is another predictive law or, more accurately, a rule of thumb which originates in the United States and which only applies when an election is a two-horse race rather than one involving several parties/candidates. It is more soundly based than the Redskins Rule (see above). The Incumbent Rule, according to the pollsters' theory, says that:

The political incumbent will only hold onto office if late polling results are above 50% in his or her favour.

The rule was formulated in 1989 by Nick Panagakis, the president of a marketing and public-opinion research firm. Everyone knows that where two major parties have roughly equivalent slices of the voting population already committed (as with the Democrats and the Republicans in the United States), then elections can only be decided by the undecideds. Although there had been a traditional belief that undecided voters generally 'break' in favour of the incumbent, perhaps along the lines of 'better the devil you know . . .', Panagakis's research suggested the opposite. Most undecideds, he pointed out, are not straddling the fence unable to make a choice. Rather, they are undecided only in respect to the existing incumbent because they are questioning his/her period in office and, given this sceptical attitude, they tend to end up siding with the challenger. Therefore the incumbent needs to have more than a 50 per cent showing in the polls to be sure of victory. Even a healthy gap of 10 per cent in the polls, with one candidate on 50 per cent and the other on 40 per cent, will produce a result closer to 52–48 per cent in the actual election (and not the equal split of undecideds that would be represented as 45–55 per cent). Panagakis cites the old rule about what the driver can see in the rear-view mirror: 'think of an incumbent poll as one in which objects are closer than they appear.'

The Incumbent Rule has been disputed by, among others, Nate Silver who achieved national fame in 2012 when he predicted a victory for Barack Obama in the presidential election rather than Mitt Romney, who was favourite in most of the polls.

Renwick's Rule

It is not only general election results that are impatiently awaited by politicians, policy wonks, statistical geeks and, occasionally, ordinary people. The outcome of a referendum may also be significant, and none was more so for the UK than the Scottish Independence vote of September 2014. How could anyone be confident about the result before the result came in? As with the Incumbent Rule (see above), not merely the numbers but also the tendencies of polling can give clues to the final outcome.

Renwick's Rule was first invoked during a debate in the House of Lords on a proposal for a referendum on the UK's membership of the European Union. Lord Lipsey, speaking against the proposal, gave both the source and substance of the rule:

> Renwick's Rule, named after Dr Alan Renwick of Reading University, shows clearly that during a referendum campaign opinion in virtually every country in the world and in virtually every case moves towards a no vote.

In a blog entry on the Reading Politics site (dated 15 January 2014) and under the heading 'Scotland's Independence Referendum: Do We Already Know the Result?', Alan Renwick explains that opinions in a referendum are likely to be more volatile than those in a general election, since people are not tethered by party loyalty. Despite this volatility, the tendency as a campaign draws to a close is for support in favour of change to fall away while support for the status quo grows stronger. The idea of change, which might have seemed appealing at first blush, suddenly starts to look risky, even alarming. An exception to this is when the status quo is presented as being untenable, with voters being persuaded or cajoled into the belief that things simply cannot carry on as they are. Then the chances of a pro-change outcome are much higher.

Looking at the evidence of past referenda, and drawing on the movement in the polls beforehand, Alan Renwick concluded that in the case of the Scottish vote of September 2014 there was likely to be a 'comfortable majority' against independence though this depended on a competent campaign being fought by the No campaign, one which avoided certain pitfalls. In the event he was right, since the voting was 55–45 per cent against independence, not a landslide but certainly 'comfortable'.

The Buckley Rule

This is a fairly obscure US political rule which nevertheless has relevance to any internal election in which there is a decision to be made between one candidate who is ideologically sound and a second candidate of the same party who is, from the purist point of view, tainted by compromise. William F. Buckley (1925–2008) was a conservative commentator and founder of the magazine *National Review*. In the aftermath of the assassination of John F. Kennedy and during the run-up to the 1964 presidential election there was a choice of two Republican candidates to oppose Lyndon Johnson, who had stepped into the White House after being Kennedy's vice-president. The rival Republicans were Nelson Rockefeller, a multi-millionaire and political centrist, and Barry Goldwater, a right-wing senator and vehement anti-Communist. At an editorial meeting Buckley announced that his magazine would support 'the rightward most viable candidate.' This is potentially ambiguous, since at the time both Rockefeller and Goldwater were 'viable' candidates. The question remains: in a knock-out contest to decide the candidate for your side, do you vote with your head for electability, or vote with your heart for doctrinal purity? Some years later, before the 1968 election and during an interview with the *Miami News*, William Buckley clarified his point by saying that he would be 'for the most right, viable candidate *who could win*' [my italics], and predicted correctly that Richard Nixon would make an electable Republican candidate in that year. So the Buckley rule is generally formulated as:

Vote for the most right candidate who is electable.

Of course, the rule can be applied to left-of-centre voters who are faced with an internal choice, as was the Labour Party in 2010 when it had to decide in a leadership contest between the

Miliband brothers, with Ed Miliband seen as more authentically left-wing than brother David. Just how electable he was was demonstrated in the 2015 election.

The Buckley Rule seems to have held in the 1964 contest for the Republican nomination between Nelson Rockefeller and Barry Goldwater. The more right-wing candidate, Goldwater, was chosen in the primaries (after campaigning under the slogan 'In your heart you know he's right', which was spoofed by the opposition with 'In your guts, you know he's nuts.') In the event, he was defeated by Johnson in a landslide although his mere presence on the Republican ticket was widely seen as invigorating the American right and leading eventually to the victory of Ronald Reagan in the presidential election of 1979. Ironically, Goldwater's position on many subjects, though seen as 'extreme' at the time, would be rejected as not going far enough by the Tea Party and purist figures who now dominate the US Republicans.

Farley's Law

All the manipulation and predictive tweaking described above may not make much difference to the actual result in an election, or so Farley's Law suggests. Although the eponymous law was formulated for American presidential politics and although it has occasionally been broken, it still has some validity both inside and beyond the United States. James Farley (1888–1976) was the campaign manager for Franklin Roosevelt's presidential bids in 1932 and 1936. Farley therefore knew what he was talking about when he came up with the dictum that voters have already made their presidential choice by Labor Day (the US public holiday celebrated on the first Monday in September), despite the fact that the most intensive campaigning is still to occur between then and the elections of early November. Academic studies have found that partisan attachment and party loyalty predetermine most voters' choices, and that campaigning doesn't make much difference. Accordingly, Farley's Law has been stated as:

Most elections are decided before the campaign begins.

The Micromega Rule and Duverger's Law

There is a curious satirical story by the eighteenth-century French philosopher Voltaire in which a 20,000 foot-high alien from a planet circling Sirius chums up with an inhabitant of Saturn who is a mere 6,000 feet tall. Together, this little-and-large act visits earth where they are eventually able to communicate with the microscopic human beings by fashioning a gigantic speaking-tube out of thumbnail parings; from the humans the giants are amused to learn of their belief that everything in the universe had been 'made uniquely for mankind'. Voltaire's *Micromégas* (1752) is the reference point for the Micromega Rule in politics which holds that:

The large prefer the small and the small prefer the large.

In practice this means that large political parties prefer smaller assemblies, smaller electoral groups and a first-past-the-post system in which the candidate who gets the largest number of votes (which may be a long way from an absolute majority) is the single winner. By contrast, larger assemblies and electoral groups, and a system of proportional representation are likely to be more inclusive and provide space for smaller parties.

French sociologist Maurice Duverger (b. 1917) concluded that the number of major parties in a democratic state is governed by the electoral system of that state. More specifically, Duverger's Law or principle states that:

> Single-winner elections within a structure of single-member districts/constituencies tend to favour a two-party system.

In the UK this is illustrated by the control of parliament by either Labour or the Conservatives and the failure of the Liberal Democrats to have any role in national government until the Conservative-Liberal Democrat coalition of 2010. A third party can take quite a healthy share of the total vote across the country but it will be thinly spread in many places and so is unlikely to gain more than a handful of seats. Protest voting aside, people tend not to put their crosses against a candidate who they know has not a hope of winning. The United States is an even clearer example of the two-party winner-takes-all system, with the Republicans and Democrats dominating the electoral process and, in effect, taking turns to hold power.

Foreign affairs

Thomas Friedman's two laws

The First Law of Petropolitics

Rising oil prices must be a bad thing, right? They lead to inflation and can even contribute to a global financial crisis, as happened after the quadruple rise of 1973–74. A very bad thing, then, except for those countries fortunate enough to be sitting on top of untapped lakes of the stuff. Yet according to Thomas Friedman (b. 1953), an author, journalist and opinion-former in United States and global politics, rising prices may not be so good for the oil-rich nations either. Indeed, they may have a negative, regressive effect on those countries' development. In an article for *Foreign Policy* magazine written in 2006 Friedman claimed to have established a link between the price of oil and the speed and extent of political or economic reform. Using the invented term 'petrolist state'[2] to describe a country whose economy is dependent predominantly on oil production and whose government has authoritarian tendencies, Friedman formulated the following law:

The price of oil and the pace of freedom always move in opposite directions in oil-rich petrolist states.

---

[2] Thomas Friedman is careful to distinguish between the petrolist states and those countries such as Britain, Norway and the United States that have large oil reserves but which also had solid democratic institutions and diversified economies in place before the oil was discovered.

There is a lengthy converse to this First Law of Petropolitics:

The lower the price of oil, the more petrolist countries are forced to move towards a political system and a society that is more transparent, more sensitive to opposition voices, and more focused on building the legal and educational structures that will maximise their people's ability, both men and women's, to compete, start new companies, and attract investments from abroad.

In Friedman's explanation, there are several reasons why higher oil prices actually make things worse for the democratic and long-term economic health of the so-called petrolist states. Among them are the facts that their leaders can use oil revenues to buy off popular discontent (the 'bread & circuses' diversion supposedly used by the Roman emperors) and that an influx of oil wealth can reduce pressure for reform in education and dampen innovation because the country is not required to be competitive in a standard style (it doesn't have to work for its living). At the most basic level, oil revenues can enable an autocratic government to strengthen its grip by spending more on police, security, intelligence and so on.

Friedman's First Law of Petropolitics – sometimes referred to by its convenient acronym FLOP – has been attacked as simplistic or just plain wrong. He has been accused of amateurism and 'paper-napkin econometrics', as suggested by the way in which he first proposed his thesis to an editor ('I laid out my napkin and drew a graph showing how there seemed to be a rough correlation between the price of oil . . . and the pace of freedom').

At least one academic paper takes him to task for a selective use of statistics and a failure to look at oil-producing countries such as Mexico or Indonesia which would have contradicted his ideas, before concluding that 'there is no such thing as the "First Law of Petropolitics"'.

The McDonald's/Golden Arches Theory

In a column written in December 1996 for the *New York Times*, Thomas Friedman put forward the following thesis:

> No two countries that both have a McDonald's have ever fought a war against each other.

Friedman said he was being tongue-in-cheek but there was enough in the idea for him to elaborate the 'Golden Arches Theory of Conflict Prevention', arguing that when a country had reached a stage of economic development which allowed its citizens to support some outposts of McDonald's, then those citizens would surely prefer to wait in a line for burgers and fries rather than queue up to fight wars. The more serious point was that a combination of rising prosperity, economic interconnectedness and globalism lead to a reduction in the chance of warfare. A few years later in 1999 Friedman felt confident enough in the Golden Arches Theory to incorporate it in book form. That was an invitation to critics to find exceptions, even as a new millennium dawned and the naive notion of the 'end of history' – the collapse of communism and the apparent triumph of liberal democracy having marked some kind of end-point – itself collapsed. Sure enough, conflicts in the Balkans as well as those between Israel and Lebanon, and Russia and Georgia (over South Ossetia) and Ukraine (over Crimea), soon showed that selling franchised burgers on your territory did not mean that you were next in line for the Nobel Peace Prize. All the countries listed in the previous sentence have (or had) McDonald's outlets.

Nevertheless, Friedman gave a further twist to the Golden Arches Theory with the Dell Theory of Conflict Prevention, as outlined in *The World Is Flat* (2005). Using the computer that he was writing the book on, and describing the complicated transnational process by which his original order for the Dell had been fulfilled, with its many parts coming from many different nations round the world, Friedman proposed that: 'No two countries that are both part of a major global supply chain, like Dell's, will ever fight a war against each other as long as they are both part of the same global supply chain.' The reasoning behind this is that the business of manufacturing components for multinationals gives stability and security to the countries where those manufacturers are based. To take time 'off', even briefly, to go to war means that one's place in the great global supply chain is at risk of being lost. Friedman cites China and Taiwan as an example of old enemies who have allowed hostility to be outweighed by commercial benefit, since both countries have an enormous investment in electronic technologies. By contrast, countries such as Afghanistan, Pakistan, Iran and North Korea are not global suppliers of parts.

Like Friedman's petropolitics idea (see above), there is enough validity and appeal in the Golden Arches and the Dell theories for them to look good or intriguing as headlines or in books of popular theorizing. However, none seems robust enough to stand up to real academic examination or simply to survive the rush of history.

The Pottery Barn Rule

The Pottery Barn Rule is a warning which was originally to be seen in shops and which states:

> If you break it, you own it.

In other words, if you smash something in a store then that makes you liable for the cost of replacing the item, even if the damage was accidental. According to the Dictionary of Modern Proverbs, the idea dates back to at least the early 1950s when a Miami Beach gift shop displayed rows of fragile goods alongside the warning: 'If you break it, you've bought it.' The attribution to the Pottery Barn, an upmarket US chain of home furnishing stores, is mistaken, and the company was quick to point out that it carried no such 'rule'. In fact, far from enforcing such a rule, most retailers write off accidental damage because to pursue claims against customers is both bad for business as well as difficult and expensive to enforce in law.

More widely, the breakage rule can be interpreted to mean that not just the financial but the moral responsibility for putting something right lies with the individual who caused the damage in the first place. Like both the petropolitics theory and the Golden Arches Law (see above), the Pottery Barn Rule has been laid at the door of Thomas Friedman, even though it is identified most closely with Colin Powell,[3] the US secretary of state during the presidency of George W. Bush and the 2003 invasion of Iraq. Powell was a voice of caution in an administration that was, with disastrous results, gung-ho for action. At the Aspen Ideas Festival in 2007, Colin Powell described how he conveyed his doubts about invading Iraq to President Bush:

> I went to the president in August of 2002 . . . For the better part of two and a half [hours], I took him through not only the military planning that was being done in the Pentagon but . . . through the consequences of going into an Arab country and becoming the occupiers. It is said that I used the 'Pottery Barn rule.' I never did it; [Thomas] Friedman did it . . . But what I did say . . . [is that] once you break it, you are going to own it, and we're going to be responsible for 26 million people standing there looking at us. And it's going to suck up a good 40 to 50 percent of the Army for years. And it's going to take all the oxygen out of the political environment.

The converse of the Pottery Barn Rule – 'If it ain't broke, don't fix it' – sounds like an old proverb. Although not appearing in print before the mid-1970s, when quoted by a member of President

---

[3] Colin Powell also created the 40–70 rule for making difficult decisions. According to the one-time chairman of the joint chiefs of staff: 'You never make a decision with less than 40 per cent of the information. But you never wait until you have more than 70 per cent of the information. With 40 per cent of the information you are more in the dark than in the light, and so likely to make mistakes. But if you wait until you have amassed a large amount of information – over the 70 per cent – then it's probably too late and someone will have beaten you to it.' This 'information rule' can also be related to Segal's Law (see page 207).

Jimmy Carter's administration to argue against government spending on unnecessary projects, 'If it ain't broke, don't fix it' probably originated in the southern US states.

Domino Theory

Sometimes called the 'domino effect', this was a popular theory during most of the Cold War era, and was used to justify Western – that is, American – intervention in countries far distant from the United States or Europe. In its blandest and most generalized form the theory can be summed up as:

A political event or development in one country may lead to its occurrence in neighbouring ones.

The reference is to a line of dominoes, and the image was first conjured up by President Eisenhower at a press conference in 1954, where he expressed the fear that communism, originating in China, would spread to neighbouring countries. Korea had already been partitioned and the French were withdrawing from their colonial empire in southeast Asia (now Vietnam, Laos and Cambodia). Eisenhower said: 'You had broader considerations that might follow what you might call the "falling domino" principle. You had a row of dominoes set up, and you knocked over the first one, and what would happen to the last one was the certainty that it would go over very quickly.'

The Domino Theory was widely cited throughout the Vietnam War, and during later periods of communist involvement in governments and coups in Africa and South America. Cuba, in America's backyard, was frequently seen as the source of 'contagion' which if not contained might spread in accordance with the domino principle. The idea is sometimes applied in a positive sense, as in the notion that the establishment of a democratic system in one country might encourage a similar development in neighbouring ones, but usually the falling dominoes are associated with negatives such as collapsing economies, nuclear proliferation and so on.

The Madman Theory

Picture this. You are standing on the edge of a cliff and it's a long drop down. You certainly don't want to wander too close to the brink. Unfortunately, you are chained by the ankle to another person. And that is not the end of your predicament because you are taking part in a macabre game in which you will only be released if one of you admits defeat (or cries uncle, in the American expression). The person who doesn't cry uncle, the one who stays silent, will not only be rewarded with freedom but also a large prize. What do you do in response? Start clowning about and dancing around, all the time getting closer and closer to the cliff-edge in the hope that your partner will grow worried, lose his nerve and cry out? Maybe. But what would you do if you suspected that your shackled fellow was no clown but really a bit unhinged, just a touch mad, exactly the sort of person to get too close to the edge and even to throw himself – and you – off into space, just for the hell of it? Then you'd surely be the one crying uncle, and pretty quick too.

This is the cliff-edge 'game' as described by Thomas Schelling (b. 1921), an economist and an expert in game-theory. Aficionados will recognize its similarity to the Prisoner's Dilemma.[4] Schelling was one of a group of analysts at the Rand Corporation, a US think-tank where nuclear war, game theory and brinkmanship were the subjects of dispassionate study during the Cold War period. Henry Kissinger, later secretary of state under President Nixon, was also a consultant at Rand. And it was Richard Nixon together with Kissinger who formulated the 'madman theory' which can be summarized as:

> To win concessions from the other side, it may be advantageous for a leader to put on a show of being so desperate that he will behave in irrational, unpredictable ways.

The Madman Theory emerged at a time when the United States was increasingly bogged down in the Vietnam War. In the first half of 1969 alone, more than 4,500 American soldiers had died, and the peace negotiations being held in Paris had broken down.

---

[4] In the Prisoner's Dilemma, two people arrested for, say, a major theft are placed in separate cells so that they are unable to communicate with each other. A prosecutor has sufficient evidence to convict each on separate but minor charges (say, handling stolen goods) but not for the principal offence. The prosecutor makes each the same offer: 'You can confess or keep silent. It's your right. But if your partner confesses and you don't, then he will go free while you do extra time. The same in reverse, as far as you're concerned. If each of you confesses, then I'll make sure you both get reduced sentences. And if neither of you does, then I'll have to settle for a conviction on those handling charges.' The dilemma for both prisoners is that selfless or 'honourable' behaviour, in which each keeps silent, is better rewarded (though still incurring a minor punishment) than both confessing. But if one pursues self-interest by confessing and the other doesn't, then the selfish one gets the ultimate reward of freedom.

Nixon needed to do something to persuade the Soviet Union to put pressure on North Vietnam, its client state, to make concessions at the negotiating table. To that end, in late October 1969, a squadron of 18 giant Stratofortress bombers, each one equipped with nuclear weapons, was despatched to skirt around the edge of Soviet territory and probe its defences in an exercise that lasted three days. The code name for the operation was Giant Lance.

The aim of Nixon and Kissinger was to make the Soviets believe that the US President was unstable and dangerously volatile, to the extent of being prepared to consider a nuclear attack if he didn't get his own way. According to this scenario, Nixon played the bad cop in meetings with the Russian ambassador while Kissinger was the good cop, trying to persuade the Soviets that his master was 'out of control' and had to be humoured. As Nixon confided to Bob Haldeman, the White House Chief of Staff who was later imprisoned for his role in the Watergate conspiracy:

> I call it the Madman Theory, Bob. I want the North Vietnamese to believe I've reached the point where I might do anything to stop the war. We'll just slip the word to them that, 'for God's sake, you know Nixon is obsessed about communism. We can't restrain him when he's angry – and he has his hand on the nuclear button', and Ho Chi Minh [President of North Vietnam] himself will be in Paris in two days begging for peace.

Nixon enjoyed boasting of the unprecedented destructive powers at his disposal. He once told a White House dinner party: 'I could leave this room, and in 25 minutes, 70 million people would be dead.' But in the case of Vietnam, the Madman Theory didn't work and it took several more years of fighting until a peace deal was concluded in 1973. However, Nixon and Kissinger believed that their provocative posture helped persuade the Russians to begin serious negotiations over arms control. It has also been claimed that the North Vietnamese wouldn't have invaded South Vietnam in 1975 had Nixon still been president (he resigned in 1974 following the Watergate scandal), since they believed he was capable of reacting irrationally.

There are at least two major flaws in the Madman Theory: it presupposes that, however mad and convincing your play-acting is, the other side is rational enough to be frightened into surrender rather than launching a panic-stricken counter-attack; and, in the case of a 'pretend' nuclear exercise, there is always the risk of a terrible and terminal error. It is more than a coincidence that the military-political strategy which dominated the Cold War years and produced a kind of uneasy equilibrium was known as mutual assured destruction or more usually referred to by its acronym of MAD.

The White Flag Principle

This is the title of a book, first published in 1972, by Shimon Tzabar (1926–2007). A maverick, dissident figure, Tzabar was, among other things, a cartoonist, a writer, a satirist and an expert on mushrooms, which he documented and illustrated in watercolours. Despite having fought during the 1940s with the Israeli underground forces against British control of what was then Palestine, Tzabar left Israel after the Six Day War of 1967 which saw his country turn the tables on its Arab neighbours and begin the process of occupation and settlement-building, with which he profoundly disagreed. He established himself in London and produced The White Flag Principle, whose underlying thesis is:

Military defeat may produce a better postwar situation than victory.

A satirical notion, yes, but not entirely since the flourishing post-1945 histories of both Germany and Japan demonstrated that there were some advantages in a cataclysmic defeat. And Shimon Tzabar researched the subject seriously, spending a year in the British Library and annotating his findings on thousands of file cards. That *The White Flag Principle* is a satirical reverse of the standard strategic handbook is shown by Tzabar's intention to make defeat rather than victory the objective; to that end, he said, one must have a disastrous foreign policy so as to produce enemies instead of allies, and also ensure that the economy is in a mess, for strong economies tend to be associated with victories. Shimon Tzabar shows his satirical touch with such detailed subject-headings as 'Raising the white flag and, in case there is no white flag, how to make one from other flags' or 'Exercises for being able to keep your hands up without getting tired'.

Harold Macmillan's First Political Rule

Harold Macmillan (1894–1986) was prime minister for a six-year period from 1957, until he was brought down by the Profumo Scandal (see the Thirty-Year Rule). Overseeing the shrinking of British imperial power overseas and social change at home, Macmillan projected an image of unflappable calm, urbane wit and good sense. And never more so, perhaps than when he gave some advice to his successor, Alec Douglas-Home. Macmillan is supposed to have summoned the younger man – Douglas-Home was a mere sixty at the time – to his office and said: 'My dear boy, as long as you don't invade Afghanistan you'll be absolutely fine.' This has often been reduced to a pithier form in which it is referred to as Macmillan's first rule of politics. It needs no further commentary:

Never invade Afghanistan.

Chatham House Rule

This rule is named after the London mansion which houses the Royal Institute of International Affairs, the prestigious think-tank which was inaugurated in 1920 and which focuses on current affairs and global issues. The Chatham House Rule was first formulated in 1927, and in its current revised form states:

When a meeting, or part thereof, is held under the Chatham House Rule, participants are free to use the information received, but neither the identity nor the affiliation of the speaker(s), nor that of any other participant, may be revealed.

If participants to a meeting or seminar know that they will not be linked in public to particular views or comments, they are likely to speak more freely, especially if they are deviating from the official line of any institution they represent. As a result, information flows more easily and unfettered debate is possible. The 'Chatham House Rule' can be invoked by any organization which wants to keep its meetings confidential rather than absolutely secret, and if the phrase and the idea behind the rule aren't quite in general use they have certainly passed beyonds their confines inside the walls of a St James's Square mansion. A similar idea cloak of secrecy for the individual surrounds journalistic attributions for stories, gossip or background to 'a senior government source' or 'a member of the shadow cabinet'.

Home affairs

Overton Window Theory

The theory emanates from a right-wing think-tank based in Michigan and was named after Joseph P. Overton who died in a plane crash in 2003. Underlying the theory is the practical need in a democracy to sway public opinion so that, eventually, legislation can follow. In Overton's formulation, the theory runs as follows:

In a given public policy area only a relatively narrow range of potential policies will be considered politically acceptable.

This 'window' of politically acceptable options is primarily defined not by what politicians prefer, but rather by what they believe they can support and still win re-election.

Overton envisaged a spectrum or a yardstick, set vertically so as to get away from the old left/right-wing dichotomy, with policies arranged from the bottom (least free from government intervention/regulation) to the top (most free of the government). At any given moment, a batch of policies on the spectrum will fall within the 'window of political possibility', and, as Overton saw it, the job of shifting the window falls not so much to politicians – who tend to prefer safe choices and don't want to upset their constituencies – but to pressure groups, think-tanks and the like which will prepare the ground through a process of education, persuasion and propaganda until what had once seemed unacceptable becomes normal. The stages have been characterized as to the shift from what was once 'unthinkable' to 'radical' to 'acceptable' to 'sensible' to 'popular' to, ultimately, 'policy'.

The history of the last few decades suggests that the Overton Window Theory has some validity. In the UK the Thatcher 'revolution' of the 1980s was prepared for by think-tanks such as the Centre for Policy Studies which advocated privatization and deregulation. Under their influence, ideas previously considered unthinkable such as the privatization of parts of the prison or probation service became all too thinkable.

Similarly in the United States, the influence of free-market think-tanks promotes a pro-business, deregulated environment (while decrying any 'green' measures or redistributive taxes that would improve the environment we actually live in) and so helps to mould public opinion.

Director's Law

Aaron Director (1901–2004) was an economics professor at Chicago University, an academic centre espousing the free-market monetarist policies which dominated politics and economics in the 1980s and which have had such a benign impact round the world ever since. Director's Law, in effect, suggests that redistribution – the idea of shifting resources in society from those who have plenty to those who have less – doesn't work as it's supposed to. According to Director:

> Public expenditure is made primarily for the benefit of the middle class, and financed in large part by taxes which are borne in large part by the poor and the rich.

There are various reasons why this should be so. First, those at the bottom of the social pyramid tend not to exercise their voting rights as frequently as the average middle-income, middle-class citizen. Secondly, governments don't simply shift cash around in a vacuum but respond to pressure groups and organized social sectors in which the middle classes are disproportionately represented. And, finally, the very existence of charitable enterprises focused on alleviating poverty, helping those in need, and so on, usually creates a demand for the services, experience and employment, whether paid or voluntary, of those from the middle class.

Olson's Law

This law/observation from US academic and economist Mancur Olson (1932–98) falls somewhere in the adjoining fields of economics, political science and sociology. In his influential book *The Logic of Collective Action* (1965) Mancur Olson – the Mancur, with a soft 'c', was a local name of mysterious and seemingly Arabic origin in the prairie state of North Dakota where he grew up – looked at the balance between pressure groups, incentives to action and the wider public interest. Olson's Law, baldly stated, looks rather abstruse but in fact has large implications for the way society operates:

> The larger the group, the further it will fall short of providing an optimal amount of collective good.

At the time the law seemed to contradict the common-sense view of how things worked in free-market democratic societies, where the majority – or the bigger pressure group – would always hold the whip hand. Not when it came to producers and consumers, according to Olson. For example, it makes sense for a group of car manufacturers to join together to lobby governments for measures such as tax breaks or less onerous pollution regulations, since the benefit for each manufacturer will be substantial and obvious. The self-interested organization of a handful of companies so that they act together for shared advantage is straightforward. But organizing millions of drivers to fight back against terms which are unfavourable to them or, more widely, to society as a whole is a much harder task. Olson identified this as the 'free rider' problem, whereby people will rely on others to do the work, even if that 'work' is no more than contributing a bit of time or money to a consumers' association. In such a situation, many will feel that there is no strong personal gain or advantage to them from joining the group but rather a sense that their contributions are so small, individually, as to be irrelevant to the outcome.

Broken Window Theory

The Broken Window Theory was highly influential in US policing and criminology circles in the last two decades of the twentieth century and, although not universally accepted, it is still regarded as having some validity. Indeed, in 2011, Prime Minister David Cameron's wish to appoint Bill Bratton, a one-time police chief in New York and Los Angeles and someone closely identified with the 'broken window theory', as the metropolitan police commissioner for London was overruled by Theresa May, the home secretary, on the grounds that such a senior figure should be a British citizen. There is no set formulation for the Broken Window Theory but it can be expressed as follows:

Ignoring minor criminal damage and even non-criminal acts of public rowdiness and misbehaviour can affect people's attitudes and morale in a given area and lead to a rise in crime there.

This argument was the brainchild of two social scientists, James Q. Wilson[5] and George L. Kelling, who in an article titled 'Broken Windows' in the March 1982 edition of *The Atlantic Monthly* (available online) made the following observations:

> Social psychologists and police officers tend to agree that if a window in a building is broken and is left unrepaired, all the rest of the windows will soon be broken. This is as true in nice neighborhoods as in rundown ones. Window-breaking does not necessarily occur on a large scale because some areas are inhabited by determined window-breakers whereas others are populated by window-lovers; rather, one unrepaired broken window is a signal that no one cares, and so breaking more windows costs nothing. (It has always been fun.)

Wilson and Kelling cited a 1969 experiment by a Stanford psychologist in which a car, minus licence plates and with its hood (aka bonnet) up, was 'abandoned' in New York's Bronx, at the time a rougher district than it is now, while a car in a similar condition was left in upmarket Palo Alto in California (the city is home to Stanford University). It took ten minutes for the Bronx

---

[5] When he was Professor of Government at Harvard, James Quinn Wilson (1931–2012) also formulated two laws on research in the social sciences and its relationship to policy, laws which are cynical or realistic depending on one's viewpoint:

First Law: All policy interventions in social problems produce the intended effect – if the research is carried out by those implementing policies or their friends.

Second Law: No policy interventions in social problems produces the intended effect – if the research is carried out by independent third parties, especially those sceptical of the policy.

car to be stripped of its radiator and battery and, within 24 hours, everything of value had been taken, after which the vehicle was comprehensively trashed. By contrast, the Palo Alto automobile was left untouched for a week; to provoke things, the Stanford experimenter took a sledgehammer to it, and soon that car too had been thoroughly vandalized. The authors' conclusion is that 'vandalism can occur anywhere once communal barriers – the sense of mutual regard and the obligations of civility – are lowered by actions that seem to signal that "no one cares"'.

Hence, the importance of repairing that single broken window or dealing promptly with apparently minor incidents of public rowdiness so as to discourage a local mindset which tolerates low-level damage and disorder, as well as to calm the apprehension and fear which often arise from such things.

Moynihan's two laws

1. Daniel Patrick Moynihan (1927–2003), was a member of four US presidential administrations, beginning with John F. Kennedy's, and later was elected senator for New York, where he was succeeded in 2001 by Hilary Clinton. Moynihan was a Democrat, although he did not always agree with the liberal wing of his party. An academic, he was also capable of a pithy summation of what he saw as bias, especially where it occurred on the left, as in this observation which is known as Moynihan's Law:

The amount of violations of human rights in a country is always an inverse function of the amount of complaints about human rights violations heard from there. The greater the number of complaints being aired, the better protected are human rights in that country.

Along the same lines was his comment: 'If the newspapers of a country are filled with good news, the jails of that country will be filled with good people.'

2. Moynihan also coined another and more curious law, one seemingly made in a facetious spirit but containing a serious point. In an article for the *New York Times* published in February 1992, he recounted a talk he'd recently given to fellow Democrats in which he argued 'yet again' that there was no significant connection between school expenditure and pupil achievement. But he uncovered another and much stronger correlation – Moynihan was a social scientist and knew his way around statistics – and it was one between geographical whereabouts and eighth-grade exam scores. The further a state capital was from the Canadian border, the lower its test scores. So the Senator formulated what's been called Moynihan's Law of Proximity to the Canadian Border:

If you would improve your state's math scores, move your state closer to the Canadian border.

He added that the remedy was obvious: 'Disadvantaged states should establish summer capitals in the Thousand Islands of the St. Lawrence River, which happens to include New York State territory bordering on French-speaking Quebec.'

The application of Moynihan's Canadian border law has been broadened beyond the field of education to suggest that the further north a state lies, the fewer social problems it will have. The notion was supported by a 2011 report from the Australia-based Institute for Economics and Peace which found that the most 'peaceful' US states were Maine, New Hampshire and Vermont while the least peaceful was Louisiana.

Robert Conquest's Three Laws of Politics

Robert Conquest (b. 1917) is a historian whose best known work, *The Great Terror* (1968), analyzed the purges carried out during the 1930s in the Soviet Union under Stalin. The deaths resulting from state terror and from famine ran into millions, Conquest estimated, and his conclusions came at a time when there was still a tendency among some intellectuals in the west to look at the Soviet Union through pink-tinted glasses. He had no patience with those who claimed that Stalin was merely an aberration from some noble experiment in human betterment. Conquest is also a science-fiction aficionado who, with his friend Kingsley Amis, compiled SF anthologies; they wrote a comic novel together, *The Egyptologists* (the title is deliberately misleading). And he is a poet. Conquest combined his penchant for limericks and no-nonsense anti-communism in the following:

There was a great Marxist called Lenin
Who did two or three million men in.

That's a lot to have done in.

But where he did one in,

that grand Marxist Stalin did ten in.

And Conquest's wily conservative position is well shown by his Three Laws of Politics:

1   Everyone is conservative about what he knows best.

2   Any organization not explicitly right-wing sooner or later becomes left-wing.

3   The simplest way to explain the behaviour of any bureaucratic organization is to assume that it is controlled by a cabal of its enemies.

Conquest cited the Church of England and Amnesty International as examples of the Second Law. Of the Third, he observed that a bureaucracy sometimes actually is controlled by a secret cabal of its enemies, for example the postwar British secret service during the era of Kim Philby and the other spies from the so-called Cambridge ring.

Rawnsley's rules of politics

Andrew Rawnsley, political commentator for the *Observer* newspaper, always makes good reading on a Sunday. In an article pointing out that the public are often wrong – in this particular case wrong in some of their perceptions of the leader of the Labour Party – he notes that, unfair as this may be, the wrongness of the public doesn't matter. Along the lines of the old saying 'The customer is always . . .', Rawnsley lays down two rules:

Rule number one of politics: the voter is always right.

Rule number two: when the voter is wrong, the voter is still right.

Broder's Law

The US political columnist and pundit David Broder (1929–2011) made the observation below in *The Washington Post*, and it has sometimes been referred to as Broder's Law or Rule. As well as the US presidency, it applies to many non-political struggles to reach the top of some greasy pole:

Anybody that wants the presidency so much that he'll spend two years organising and campaigning for it is not to be trusted with the office.

Corwin's Law

Thomas Corwin (1794–1865) was an American politician and lawyer, serving as Senator for Ohio and briefly as governor for the state. Noted for his quick wit and skill in debate, he maintained that a successful candidate for office needed a serious demeanour since the 'world looks up to the teacher and down upon the clown [though] in nine cases out of ten, the clown is the better fellow of the two'.

Corwin's Law, which like Broder's Law (see above) is surely applicable to many fields beyond politics, states:

If you would succeed in life, you must be solemn as an ass. All the great monuments on earth have been built to solemn asses.

Utley's Law

This was coined by the journalist Dominic Lawson and named in honour of his one-time assistant, Virginia Utley, who had worked as secretary to various MPs at Westminster. Lawson liked her observation well enough not only to turn it into a law but to refer to it in at least two newspaper articles (*Independent*, 23 March 2010; *Daily Mail*, 8 December 2013). Virginia Utley's view was that:

> Those MPs who had the best public image as kind and caring were complete nightmares as employers, while those who had a public reputation as hard and unfeeling were absolute joys to work for.

Utley's Law is a variant on the 'don't judge a book by its cover' saying. For a conservative-learning writer such as Dominic Lawson, whose father is Nigel Lawson, Chancellor of the Exchequer under Margaret Thatcher, it must be pleasing to have anecdotal evidence that those with a reputation for being 'hard and unfeeling' are capable of being nice and considerate to their staff. Lawson also cites Mrs Thatcher's well-known concern for those who worked directly for her. The same has been said about Ronald Reagan and George W. Bush's treatment of their staff in the White House, even as Democratic presidents tend to come off less favourably. More generally, in the United States, some research has indicated that Republican voters give more time and money to charities than Democrats.

The Thirty-Year Rule

This law/rule, or a version of it, applies in several democracies, and reflects a compromise between a government's natural inclination to secrecy and the public's right to know. The right to know after thirty years, that is. In the UK, the rule applies to discussions in Cabinet and states that:

Records of cabinet meetings are confidential documents and only transferred to the National Archives after 30 years – the 30-year rule. At this point most material is released to the public.

Although some 'sensitive' material can be withheld for much longer,[6] a move has begun to shorten the gap. With the government deciding to release two years' worth of files every year since 2013, by 2022 the Thirty-Year Rule will have turned into the twenty-year rule. In addition, under the Freedom of Information Act introduced by Tony Blair, the public has the right to obtain information from government and other official

---

[6] One of six files relating to the Profumo scandal of 1963 remains sealed at the National Archives in Kew and will not be made public until at least 2046. It is believed to contain depositions and witness statements about people whose names were not brought up publicly during Stephen Ward's trial. Ward was linked to John Profumo, the Secretary of State for War, and committed suicide before an almost inevitable conviction for living on immoral earnings. When in 2013 Andrew Lloyd-Webber, the creator of a short-lived musical about Stephen Ward, raised the question in the House of Lords of why this particular file (number 4/4140) was still suppressed he was told by a government minister that it contained 'sensitive information related to people still living'. The speculation is that it involves a member of the royal family. The certainty is that, by 2046, everybody involved will be long dead (See also the Thirty-Year Rule in Science.).

bodies even though ministers still have powers to prevent certain files reaching the public domain (e.g. cabinet discussions on Scottish and Welsh devolution, and on the invasion of Iraq). In retrospect Blair was far from proud of what many people saw as a progressive and necessary move. In his autobiography he wrote of his role in pushing through the Freedom of Information Act: 'You idiot. You naive, foolish, irresponsible nincompoop. There is really no description of stupidity, no matter how vivid, that is adequate. I quake at the imbecility of it.' Blair's self-flagellation may have been prompted by the fact that among the embarrassing, if minor, information disclosed from his time in office were the fulsome congratulations sent to President George W. Bush on his first election win, the many phone conversations he enjoyed with Rupert Murdoch, and even discussions over a Blair guest appearance on 'The Simpsons'.

During World War II, emergency legislation produced the 'Fourteen Day Rule' which prohibited broadcast discussion of any subject that was due to be debated in parliament during the following fortnight. Since parliamentary business was fixed week by week, the Fourteen-Day Rule effectively precluded any radio discussion of anything in the news. It was an effective way of killing off dissent and speculation. The Rule was not withdrawn until after the Suez Crisis of 1956.

Someone or other's Ten-Day Rule

The ten-day political rule has frequently been attributed to Alastair Campbell. According to Tony Blair's spin doctor and eminence grise, when a government minister or public official is in difficulties, usually because of a personal scandal, then the following rule operates:

If you're on the front pages of newspapers for 10 days, then you've had it.

The length of time sufficient to stymy a political career varies, with nine, eleven and twelve days being cited in different versions. In an entry on his blog for September 2010 and under the heading 'My golden rule on frenzy survival lost in mists of time', Alastair Campbell claimed that, if he did make the remark, he could not remember either the occasion or the context. Somehow, this act of forgetting is more plausible than an outright denial. Campbell now says that no rule apples to the survivability of ministers during a media frenzy, since everything depends on the prevailing circumstances.

Different accounts have the spin doctors round Bill Clinton being the originators of the ten-day rule. This was their estimate of how long the media would stick with a single story before boredom set in. If the frenzy goes on beyond the standard ten/ eleven days then there are only two methods of calming it: a massive distraction such as an international crisis or the threat of war, or a very public act of contrition from the guilty party involving an apology, a confession or a resignation (or all three).

Cock-Up Theory versus Conspiracy Theory

This item appears in the Politics section because it seems a natural home for the cock-up and its entertaining ramifications.

According to Bernard Ingham, who was press secretary to
Margaret Thatcher during her premiership: 'Many journalists
have fallen for the conspiracy theory of government. I do assure
you that they would produce more accurate work if they adhered
to the cock-up theory.' Cock-up, in the sense of a blunder or failure,
seems to be a piece of service slang which emerged during or
shortly after World War II. As a full-fledged Theory it is confined
to British English even if it has a worldwide applicability, and can
be related to concepts such as Hanlon's Razor (see under Sutton's
Law). In popular use, and as in Ingham's remark, the Cock-up
Theory of history is usually opposed to the Conspiracy Theory of
history. Put simply, the Cock-up Theory tells us that:

> Disasters, misfortunes and setbacks are not the result of plotting
> by malign and powerful agencies but rather the product of
> human error and incompetence or simple bad luck.

There is, of course, a cross-over between the conspiracy and the
cock-up, as the first slips disastrously into the second. The killing
of Abraham Lincoln in April 1865 was the result of a successful
conspiracy while the conspiratorial attempt to kill Adolf Hitler
in the July 1944 plot was a tragic cock-up. The break-in at the
Watergate Building in Washington was part of an elaborate
conspiracy to guarantee the re-election of President Nixon in
1972, but what followed, with the apprehension of the burglars
and the increasingly tortuous attempts at a cover-up, was a cock-
up on a large if not supersize scale. And one of the key cock-up
versus conspiracy moments in the last quarter of the century
occurred in 1997 when Princess Diana, Dodi Fayed and their

driver were killed in a car crash in a Paris underpass. Plenty of people have made hay (and money) with their speculations that this was no accident/cock-up but an assassination conspiracy organized by a whole range of individuals or covert groups. On a more mundane level, any policy slip or misstep by those in power may be attributed not to human fallibility but to a cleverness which serves some hidden purpose and which is the more ingenious because it comes masquerading as incompetence. This then is the Conspiracy Theory, which can be defined as:

> The belief that events, especially those which are sinister or sensational, are caused or orchestrated by the deliberate action of an agency or a conspiracy between several agencies, typically secret ones and almost invariably those connected to the state. Such conspiracies are intended to blind people to the truth or to manipulate them towards beliefs which are useful to the covert agencies.

Before the arrival of the Internet, the United States provided the most fertile and familiar ground for conspiracy theories and theorizers, perhaps because of that country's wide spectrum of opinions and an enshrined tolerance of free speech. Some of the most tenacious delusions are associated with the United States and its recent history: that Lee Harvey Oswald was the fall guy for the assassination of JFK, that the moon landings were faked, that the 9/11 attack was an inside job arranged by the government. In each of these cases there is no Cock-up Theory to oppose the conspiracy idea, and so the conspiracists would say that the conspiracies have worked well since most people accept the official version (that Oswald acted alone, that the moon landings took place in reality, that the Twin Towers were brought down by an external terrorist group). Now the web has given an immeasurable and global boost to the conspiracy theorist, with the result that he – and it is mostly a he rather than a she – exists in his many millions around the world. To dabble in conspiracy theories is to dip one's toe in an almost illimitable sea of human credulity. Better not go there. They're all rubbish. Except for this one . . . and, oh, maybe that one . . . and how about. . . .?

2

Economics

There are more unofficial laws in economics than in almost any other field of human activity. Some of them are soundly based and, because of that, have grown to have a general application outside a specialist field (e.g. the law of unintended consequences or the law of diminishing returns) while others reflect complex mathematical calculations. But there are quite a few which are no more than quirky observations or insiderish-sounding tips on getting rich quick – or, at least, avoiding getting poor fast. Let's start with the more earnest ones.

The serious stuff

The law of unintended consequences

The law of unintended consequences covers almost every area of human activity and there are countless examples of this law doing its work, generally of a malign variety. It has, as far as I know, never been formulated in the style of a scientific law but can be expressed along these lines:

The purposive actions of individuals, and especially those of governments and other authorities, always have effects which have not been foreseen or intended.

This law is easier to understand in action than in theory. Take those various communities in the United States which, with the best of green intentions, decided to replace old-fashioned traffic-light bulbs with more energy-efficient ones. What no one had foreseen was that even if the previous bulbs didn't work with optimal eco-efficiency they nevertheless put out enough heat to melt any snow that fell on them. The new LED bulbs are more efficient and therefore waste less heat. As an unintended consequence the snow stays on the lights and the signal is obscured. A number of accidents have been blamed for this, and at least one death. Another traffic example: although mandatory seat belts have made drivers and their passengers safer in the UK, there has been an increase in what are called out-of-car casualties (i.e. pedestrians and cyclists). One explanation is that because drivers feel more secure with seat belts, and other safety equipment such as air-bags, they are tempted to drive more aggressively.

More positive examples of the paradoxical effect of the law of unintended consequences include the way in which areas of the British countryside set aside for army training and gunnery practice – at Lulworth in Dorset, for example, or on Salisbury Plain –

have, paradoxically, become safe havens. Not for humans but for wildlife because public access is controlled and because there has been virtually no development or exploitation of the land. Similarly, sunken ships can become artificial reefs for underwater life.

At bottom, this is a law intimately tied up with economics. The famous 'invisible hand' metaphor, created by the philosopher and economist Adam Smith (1723–90), is an example of the law of unintended consequences in a positive sense. According to Smith, each person by seeking only his own gain 'is led by an invisible hand to promote an end which was no part of his intention', that end being the public interest. For Smith the individual's desire to do well by himself produces results such as competition, higher standards and lower prices, which are of benefit to all ('It is not from the benevolence of the butcher, or the baker, that we expect our dinner, but from regard to their own self interest'). Unsurprisingly, the same argument and the 'invisible hand' metaphor are favoured by those on the political right who dislike government regulation or 'interference' in the operation of the market. Conversely, by the same unintended-consequences law and according to some economists, higher taxes may lead to lower revenues because they supposedly encourage tax avoidance, discourage enterprise and may even cause a bird-like migration of wealthy entrepreneurs to places where they pay less.

The law of unintended consequences operates on three levels. The first, and most rare, is a benign one in which actions have unforeseen good effects, in the way that untended areas such as firing ranges or railway banks may provide wild-life habitats and refuges. On the second level a beneficial outcome will be balanced or offset by a negative, unexpected result (the seat-belt example). The worst case of all is when some action designed to improve a situation actually makes it worse. The so-called cobra effect falls into this category and, even if it is apocryphal, the story is worth repeating. During the colonial era of British rule in India, the government offered a bounty on every cobra killed in Delhi. When the authorities became aware that some people were breeding and killing cobras solely for the money they withdrew the bounty. The breeders then released their worthless snakes into the wild, causing an increase in the snake population greater than would have occurred if there had never been a bounty scheme in the first place. A similar situation prevailed in the Vietnamese capital Hanoi during French colonial rule, when the authorities offered a bounty for every rat's tail. But a mutilated rat is not necessarily a dead one, and the city was soon fuller than ever with creatures that had been captured, de-tailed and released to carry on with breeding more generations and more bounty.

It was the American sociologist Robert K. Merton who popularized the concept of unintended consequences in an influential article titled 'The Unanticipated Consequences of Purposive Social Action' (1936). Merton identified five sources of unforeseen consequences, of which the first two, ignorance and error, were the most common. A similar idea was expressed in pithy fashion by US journalist and commentator, Eric Sevareid, who pronounced on CBS news that 'The chief cause of problems is solutions', a formulation known as Sevareid's Law. In a more familiar style, the concept of unintended consequences can be connected to sod's/Murphy's Law and to proverbial sayings such as 'The road to hell is paved with good intentions.' Perhaps ironically, Robert Merton, who died in 2003, never finished the book on unanticipated consequences which he announced he was going to write in the original 1936 article, despite having worked on it for sixty years.

The law of diminishing returns

Like the law of unintended consequences (see above) the law of diminishing returns has its origins in the world of economics, but long ago spilled over into daily life.

Just as familiar as the experience of plans which go wrong in a perverse and self-defeating way (the law of unintended consequences) is the discovery that some process may yield progressively smaller increases – in terms of profit or pleasure – despite a greater expenditure of time, money or effort being put into it (the law of diminishing returns). Expressed in specifically economic terms, the law says:

> As quantities of one variable factor are increased, while other factor inputs remain constant, all things being equal, a point is reached beyond which the addition of one more unit of the variable factor will result in a diminishing rate of return and the marginal physical product will fall.

Or, to put it more simply, you can have too much of a good thing. An example which is often used to illustrate the idea of diminishing returns is that of the farmer who buys fertilizer to increase the yield of his crops. The first applications of the fertilizer will produce a burst of growth as compared to the unfertilized state. Further doses will increase the yield too, but at a decreasing rate. Then there comes a point when the cost of spreading more of the stuff is greater than the profit from the small increases of yield that result – and a tipping-point occurs after that when yields will actually go down because the soil and crops have been harmed by excessive fertilizer use. A similar calculation operates in a workplace, from cafe to factory floor. More workers may mean more productivity at first but the return from adding the extra worker(s) will diminish over time because of overcrowding, problems of supervision, inefficiency and so on, as long as the original work space/conditions/ machinery remain unchanged. This last point – the 'while other factor inputs remain constant' bit of the law as quoted above – is important. If the farmer buys more land or the cafe-owner builds a bigger kitchen, then it may be necessary and profitable for him or her to buy more fertilizer/hire more cooks – until the law of diminishing returns kicks in again.

The law applies in other areas which have nothing to do with economics. Consumption of alcohol or ice-cream, promises by politicians, swearing on telly, big explosions or increasingly gruesome horror in films – all of them are subject to the law of diminishing returns.

Gresham's Law

Sir Thomas Gresham (1519–79) was a court financier under several monarchs, including Elizabeth I. In a letter of 1558 urging her to restore the country's debased coinage, he made several observations such as 'good and bad coin cannot circulate together.' Long after Gresham's death these were simplified into a five-word formula:

Bad money drives out good.

Although the meaning behind the proverbial-style utterance had already been expressed by earlier scholars such as the mathematician and astronomer Nicolaus Copernicus (1473– 1543), it took three centuries for 'Bad money drives out good' to be christened Gresham's Law by H. D. Macleod, a nineteenth-century Scottish economist. Incidentally, the attribution of a law to someone who didn't actually create it is itself covered by Stigler's Law of Eponomy (see page 128).

An illustration of Gresham's Law occurred retrospectively during the reign of Elizabeth I's father, Henry VIII, when the coinage was officially 'debased' on several occasions (a coin is debased when its face value stays the same but either the weight is reduced or the ratio of metals in the alloy is changed, i.e. by using less silver or gold and more copper). Anyone lucky enough to have a store of 'old' coins with a relatively high proportion of precious metal alongside a heap of the 'new' ones containing more copper would almost inevitably choose to use the debased money, while hoarding the ones with a higher intrinsic value. During the French Revolution, the government introduced paper notes known as assignats and threatened the death penalty against anyone who wouldn't trade the notes at their face value. This drove out of use the silver écu, which had previously circulated. Even without the death penalty threat this would have happened since the écu had a real intrinsic value – it could be melted down, it could be traded in areas outside France – as opposed to the merely notional worth of the assignats. In this way, 'bad' money will drive the 'good' out of circulation.

Now that old-style coinage and even banknotes are going the way of bartering with animal skins or cowrie shells, Gresham's Law may seem redundant. But it has been given a fresh life outside the world of finance to cover those many situations in which an inferior product or practice will expel a superior one. Thus Roy Hattersley writes that 'there is a Gresham's law of politics which too often results in the meanness of mind driving out the generous impulse' or Christopher Hitchens claims 'The "royal" theme operates with the intensity of Gresham's Law in this sector [the British press], encouraging laziness and sentimentality and salacity by making it too easy to fill page upon page with brainless twaddle, and encouraging contempt for the readership that makes itself such an easy target.'

Investment and marketing tips

Greater Fool theory

This is one of those economic/market theories which suggests that speculation is essentially a business for idiots. The Greater Fool theory maintains that:

Any price, no matter how unrealistic, can be justified if the buyer believes that there is another buyer who will pay an even higher price for the same item.

In rising (bull) markets, things that are fashionable, like the newest Internet startup company, or in short supply, like desirable housing in desirable places, can rapidly acquire a value which is out of proportion to their 'true' worth. Despite this, it may be worth buying in the expectation that someone else, otherwise known as the bigger or greater fool, will pay you more money than you paid in the first place. If caution holds you back, then you will lose out for as long as the item continues to rise in price. And even though the little whisper of common sense tells you that bubbles burst, that there will be tears before bedtime and so on, a sustained period of rising prices often leads to the belief that we are uniquely blessed because 'it's different this time'. Not so; all good things must come to an end and prices will eventually stop rising and, probably, go down. Then there are no buyers. The well of greater fools has run dry. Until the market starts to edge up again. The Greater Fool theory applies especially to the art market because it trades in objects which have little or no intrinsic worth and are valuable only through a kind of mass assessment which combines financial speculation with aesthetic appreciation, usually with a spoonful of fashion tipped in.
(See also Stein's Law below.)

Stein's Law

Herb Stein (1916–99) was an economics adviser under US presidents Nixon and Ford. He formulated the law which is named after him and which states:

If something cannot go on forever, it will stop.

At first glance this tautologous statement doesn't look as though it's worth making, let alone earning the accolade of being an economic 'iron rule'. But it operates as a warning about taking precipitate action against a situation – the example Stein himself gave was a deficit in the balance of payments – which is bound to end of its own accord sooner or later. Stein's Law is a useful, but generally disregarded, caution for those who believe that a stock-market trend like the dot-com boom of the late 1990s or a buoyant market in house prices will, through some magical gravity-defying process, go on forever. By stressing that everything is provisional and transient, the Law undermines dogmatic statements such as 'It's different this time' (a phrase once described as 'the four most dangerous words in investment') or Gordon Brown's boast of abolishing boom-and-bust, a claim often made in the run-up to the global financial meltdown which began in 2007. In addition, Stein's Law is a handy tool for right-wing commentators in the United States who like to point out that what they call the 'entitlement culture' can't go on expanding forever, usually as prologue to a demand for cutbacks now.

Warren Buffet's Rules

Warren Buffet (b1930), the largest shareholder and CEO of Berkshire Hathaway, is a famous US investor, money-maker, philanthropist and business guru (one of his nicknames is the Sage of Omaha). A flavour of Buffet's often unconventional advice can be detected in his two cardinal rules:

1   Never lose money.

2   Don't forget Rule Number one.

In 2011 Warren Buffet contributed to the debate about widening income inequality by saying that it was wrong that wealthy people like him should pay proportionally less in federal taxes than members of the middle- and working class. President Obama quickly adopted what he called the 'Buffet rule', requiring millionaires to pay a fair share amounting to at least 30 per cent of their income in taxes. The proposal stumbled over Republican opposition in the Senate. Buffet returned to the issue in 2013, saying that was still paying tax at a lower rate than his secretary.

Random Walk Theory

This is another of those investment theories which is consoling to the non-expert and irritating to the financial analysts and specialists since it suggests that they are wasting their time (and your money). Random Walk Theory states that:

> The past movement or direction of the price of a stock or the overall market cannot be used to predict its future movement.[1]

Although the idea had been around for many years, it was developed in its current form by Burton Malkiel in *A Random Walk Down Wall Street* (1973). Malkiel (b. 1932), a businessman and academic, describes in the book how he tried to counter the idea that stocks are like fullbacks (in American football) who, if they gain some

---

[1] A version of random walk theory appears in the small-print warnings on investment ads and prospectuses: 'Past performance is no guide to future returns' or 'Prices can go down as well as up'.

momentum, are expected to 'carry on for a long gain'. Observing that this is not the case, Malkiel recounted an experiment he devised with his Princeton students. They drew graphs showing the movement of a notional piece of stock, marking it up or down at the close of each day. But the movement in either direction was determined by nothing more than the tossing of a coin, with heads for half a point higher, tails for half a point lower. Despite being totally random products, since the coin has an equal chance of coming down heads or tails each time, the charts which resulted looked remarkably convincing, and even displayed illusory patterns and signs of cycles of activity. When Malkiel showed one of the graphs to a friend, he asked what company it represented and said, 'We've got to buy immediately. This pattern's a classic. There's no question the stock will be up 15 points next week.'

Even if market movements are not absolutely random, Malkiel maintained that there was enough validity in the theory for an investor not to continuously chop and change his holdings in the hope of playing the market and outdoing the investor who simply holds on to a portfolio for the long term (since the long-run tendency of the market is upward).

Odd Lot Theory

In US stock market terminology an 'odd lot' is a small number of shares, and the odd-lotters are those individuals who deal in them. Such small-time dealers are not highly regarded, at least by the big boys. According to the *New York Times*: 'Odd-lot investors, the small-fry who buy and sell fewer than 100 shares, have a reputation for doing the wrong thing.' And it's this reputation for doing the wrong thing which is at the root of the Odd Lot Theory which suggests the following investment strategy:

An investor can make a profit by doing the opposite of whatever the odd-lotters are doing.

So if the small-fry are selling/buying a particular stock, then it's time for the real players to do the reverse and buy/sell. There is a patronizing grain of truth in the theory, which implies that those unsophisticated odd-lotters are likely to be victims of bad timing. Being both badly informed and innately cautious, they will always buy when the market has reached its peak or sell when it has touched bottom. But there was never much supporting evidence for it and, if it was ever much observed, the Odd Lot theory has fallen out of favour in an era when individual investors tend to put their money into mutual funds.

Rational Expectations Theory

Some economic ideas, such as the Greater Fool or the Odd Lot theories, suggest that playing the markets is a business which is best left either to mugs or to the very clever. The Rational Expectations Theory (RET), by contrast, is reassuring in both its name and its operation. Since its formulation in the early 1960s the RET has been expressed in various ways but is most easily summarized as the belief that:

People make economic choices based on a rational outlook · formed by all the information which is available to them in the present and the experiences they have had in the past.

The theory operates from the point of view of both producers and consumers. For example, how many acres farmers give to a particular crop depends on their expectation of the money they will get by selling that crop, and their decision will be based on the way they expect prices to go in future which, in turn, will be based on patterns they have discerned in the past. On the other side of the fence, if a sufficient number of consumers hold off from buying something because they believe its price will soon fall, then demand for that product slackens and the price is indeed likely to go down. The RET is not infallible, since predictive expectations can be overturned by surprise events, but it holds that outcomes will not be not systematically different – that is, not different on a regular or predictable pattern – from what people expect them to be.

The Underpant Gnomes theory of marketing

Like the Eddie Murphy Rule (see below), this comes from an unexpected source. In fact, from the seventeenth episode of the second season of the US animated series *South Park*. In it Stan and the rest of the gang are given a presentation by the underground gnomes on how to achieve business success by capitalizing on the underpants which they (the gnomes) steal. These are the three stages in the gnomes' planning:

Phase 1: Collect Underpants

Phase 2: ?

Phase 3: Profit

The Gnomes' theory has been used satirically or in cautionary style to apply to plenty of business models which haven't been properly thought through, especially the online ones. In these versions the plan goes: Phase One: Build a great website and attract plenty of visitors; Phase Two: ?; Phase 3: Profit.

Warning signs and cautionary tales

Cockroach Theory

The world of high finance and the stock market is home to a small menagerie, whether in the shape of large beasts such as the bulls and bears that signify a rising and a falling market, respectively, or the smaller creatures such as lame ducks and dead cats (a 'dead cat bounce' is a temporary and misleading rally in the price of falling stock).

Circling above these are the so-called vulture funds, companies that buy up large-scale debt at a discount and then try to squeeze a profit from the distressed debtors. Possibly even less welcome than a vulture is another creature that no one wants to see close-up in their neighbourhood: the cockroach. This universal aversion has given rise to the Cockroach Theory which, simply stated, tells us that:

There's never just one of them.

Or, if you want it expressed more poetically, here it is in the words of Claudius in Hamlet:

When sorrows come, they come not single spies/But in battalions.

Put in more prosaic terms, the Cockroach Theory predicts that when a company reveals a piece of bad news, this is not the end of the story. More bad news is on the way. The analogy comes from the common belief that sight of a single cockroach is usually a sign that there are plenty more of them hidden close by. And the theory can apply not just to a single company but to the entire system or market. The global financial meltdown that started in 2007 might at first have seemed traceable to the misbehaviour and stupidity of a few bad banking apples bringing disrepute to the majority of their shiny cousins in the barrel – and near disaster to the rest of us. But it quickly became plain that THEY WERE ALL AT IT.

And they probably still are.

Hemline Theory

The hemline theory (sometimes called skirt-length theory) goes back nearly a hundred years and is generally accredited to George W. Taylor or to Paul Nystrom, both of them American academics and either of whom may have established a connection between skirt dimensions and economic conditions. Doubt has been cast on the attribution, however, since both men are supposed to have come up with the idea before the key event – the 1929 Wall Street Crash – which would have provided the best supporting evidence.

Anyway, with or without a founding father, the theory proposes that:

Hemlines go up with rising stock markets and drop with falling ones.

This feels right if only in an anecdotal sort of way. The mini-skirted 1960s were, after all, a period of unprecedented prosperity in the quarter century which followed the end of Word War Two, while the maxi-skirt emerged during the inflationary, oil-embargoed 1970s. In 2010 two researchers from the Erasmus School of Economics in Rotterdam put what they described as an urban legend to the test by looking at hemlines from as far back as the 1920s, distinguishing between five different lengths (from mini through cocktail dress to floor length), and correlating their rise and fall with economic statistics. Using charts, graphs and formulae, Marjolein van Baardwijk and Philip Hans Franses established that there is indeed a link between shorter skirts and better times as there is between longer skirts and bad ones, but with a lag of around three years. This explained why, in their own words, 'at present [2010], in an economic downturn, the skirts are short, as this is simply due to the fact that the economy was in a boom about three years ago (2007–2008)'.

Why this should be so is obscure. The explanation that shorter skirts mean women can show off their boom-time silk stockings while longer skirts hide depression-era hosiery might have held true in the 1920s and 30s but won't work for later periods. Maybe it is simply that tough times make for more conservative fashions while a general sense of exuberance, daring and confidence pushes up both markets and hemlines, even if the movements are not quite in synch. There are several other fashion-related pointers to economic well-being – the lipstick-index (more often bought under economic pressure because lipstick is a cheaper alternative to shoes, handbags, etc.), the tie-width indicator (skinny ties=hard times; fat ties=good times) – but so far they have not been subjected to rigorous academic analysis.

Skyscraper Index theory

This well-known indicator/predictor of storm clouds on the economic horizon has been the subject of some academic debate since it was first raised in a 1999 paper called 'The Skyscraper Index: Faulty Towers'. In fact, the fairly obvious link between the construction of tall towers and a buoyant financial situation had been made much earlier in the twentieth century, but it was Andrew Lawrence – a property analyst with a sense of humour to judge by the title of his paper – who pointed out the Babel-like hubris which is seemingly involved in erecting these grand projects.

The index shows that:

> The completion of the latest 'tallest building in the world' is a sign that a financial recession is on the way.

The prompt for Andrew Lawrence's thesis was the completion in 1998 of the Petronas Towers in Kuala Lumpur, which for six years held the record as the world's tallest buildings. At the same time large parts of south-east Asia, including Malaysia, fell victim to a regional economic crisis that became known as the Asian Contagion. Other notable examples of building pride coming immediately before a stock-market fall are the completion in New York of the Chrysler Building and the Empire State Building, in 1930 and 1931 respectively, just as the effects of the Great Depression were kicking in. Similarly, the completion of the ill-fated Twin Towers in the same city and of the Sears Roebuck Tower in Chicago, both in 1973, ushered in a period of economic insecurity and rocketing oil prices. And the latest skyscraper to sip from the poisoned chalice of 'world's tallest' is the Burj Khalifa in Dubai. Begun in 2004 and officially opened in 2010 while the world was passing through the worst economic troubles since the 1930s, this needle-like structure underwent a change of name from Burj (i.e. tower) Dubai to Burj Khalifa in honour of Sheikh Khalifa, the ruler of neighbouring Abu Dhabi, which came to the rescue of Dubai during the financial meltdown.

Skyscraper-building is essentially a speculative venture, since they are rarely constructed by the companies which will eventually occupy them and, indeed, often without committed tenants. Periods of easy money, of expanding business and improving technology – boom times – encourage the erection of tall towers. Often there's a nationalistic element, too, since possession of the 'world's tallest' is evidence of being a global player in finance and commerce. Then the speculative excitement reaches its climax, and business activity contracts even as anxiety in the financial markets prompts a decline in the relative price of buildings. So the skyscraper begun in a spirit of swagger and exhilaration as the market heads for its feverish peak will finish as a half-empty shell, a white elephant sitting on its bottom and with its trunk stretching up into space.

An interesting variant on the skyscraper index was proposed by Ian Hamilton, the CEO of a South African hedge fund.

Terming it 'crane theory', he proposed that the vision of a city skyline crowded with cranes should be not an encouragement but a deterrent to investment there. Citing Dubai, which at one stage boasted that it had half the world's building cranes, as well as Dublin in 2006–7, Hamilton argued that such a hectic programme of building, and not just of skyscrapers, was a indication that the bubble was about to burst. It is also reported that young western spies, when visiting a foreign city, are told to count the number of active cranes as a sign of economic activity.

Goodhart's Law

This started life as a law of economics coined by the British economist and academic Charles Goodhart (b. 1936). In his original formulation, it stated that: 'Any observed statistical regularity will tend to collapse once pressure is placed upon it for control purposes.' Put more simply Goodhart's Law can be summarized as:

> When a measure becomes a target, it ceases to be a good measure.

Easier to illustrate than to explain, the Law suggests that the moment you start to measure something in order to achieve a specific purpose you introduce distortions by the very act of measuring. For example, in the UK, a target of eight minutes for an ambulance to arrive on the scene of a life-threatening situation was a creditable attempt to improve services, and forms part of the starred ratings system by which the regional health services are assessed. The move led to the introduction of rapid response cars, which are quicker and easier to handle than ambulances, and so able to hit the target time more often, but which carry less equipment and fewer personnel. The result is that, although some help arrives earlier on the scene, proper treatment may still be delayed until the fully equipped ambulance turns up.

The US social scientist Donald Campbell (1916–96) pointed to a similar pattern in the field of education where the worth of (and consequent rewards given to) a pupil, a teacher or an institution may be determined by a single quantitative measure such as a batch of test scores. The higher the value placed on that measure, the more likely is the process itself to become distorted, even corrupted. Among the unintended results may be a narrowing of the curriculum, what's called 'teaching to the test' and even cases of outright cheating. A combination of Goodhart's and Campbell's Laws helps to explain why people so frequently feel baffled and frustrated when government announces that certain targets are being met, since their actual experience may be suggesting something quite different.

The Micawber principle

In Charles Dickens's novel *David Copperfield* (1850) Wilkins Micawber and his large family live in a state of chronic debt. A volatile character, Mr Micawber is either down in the dumps or planning confidently for better times 'in case anything turned up', his favourite if somewhat forlorn expression. The Micawber principle might well be that 'something will turn up', the inevitable improvement in his fortunes which he expects in the same way that people expect to win the lottery . . . one day. But Micawber's principle, as generally understood, is that the smallest difference on a balance sheet can produce diametrically opposite emotions. Just as Mrs Thatcher sometimes used the idea of a household budget as an analogy for national expenditure when she was Prime Minister, so Micawber's Principle is occasionally invoked in the word of serious economics. As Mr Micawber tells David Copperfield:

> Annual income twenty pounds, annual expenditure nineteen nineteen and six,[2] result happiness. Annual income twenty pounds, annual expenditure twenty pounds ought and six, result misery.

Dickens gives Micawber and his family a happy ending by shipping them off to Australia, where the cash-strapped optimist becomes a magistrate.

The Eddie Murphy Rule

In the aftermath of the financial meltdown of 2007–8 there were plenty of political pledges to bring in new laws and regulations

---

[2] The difference between spending just under an annual income of £20 and just over it, and therefore between Micawber's happiness and misery, is one shilling or 5p in modern currency (half a shilling or sixpence – six old pennies – represents 2.5p).

to prevent it happening again, ever. One of the oddest, at least in terms of its title, is known in the United States as the Eddie Murphy Rule. Not to be confused with the original Murphy's Law, the Eddie version says that:

A federal employee may not knowingly disseminate information which has not been made public by the government that may affect the price of a commodity or use such information in a commodity transaction.

The source is the 1983 comedy *Trading Places*, starring Eddie Murphy and Dan Aykroyd as, respectively, a street bum and a thrusting broker who exchange roles as a result of manipulation by the powerful and unscrupulous Duke brothers. Eventually realizing the trick that's been played on them, the two join forces to bring down the Dukes by using inside information, as well as a bit of theft and forgery. The surprising application of a film scenario to real life nearly thirty years later was explained by Gary Gensler, head of the Commodity Futures Trading Commission (CFTC), in testimony to Congress in March 2010:

We have recommended banning using misappropriated government information to trade in the commodity markets. In the movie 'Trading Places', starring Eddie Murphy, the Duke brothers intended to profit from trades in frozen concentrated orange juice futures contracts using an illicitly obtained and not yet public Department of Agriculture orange crop report. Characters played by Eddie Murphy and Dan Aykroyd intercept the misappropriated report and trade on it to profit and ruin the Duke brothers. In real life, using such misappropriated government information actually is not illegal under our statute. To protect our markets, we have recommended what we call the 'Eddie Murphy' rule to ban insider trading using nonpublic information misappropriated from a government source.

Sibley's Law

This is attributed to banker Nicholas Sibley, one time managing director of Jardine Fleming, and it was often quoted during the financial crisis of 2007–8 as a wry comment on the folly of throwing money at the very banks which were part of the problem in the first place. Sibley's Law states:

Giving capital to a bank is like giving a gallon of beer to a drunk. You know what will become of it, but you can't know which wall he will choose.

Working the numbers

Rule of 72

Here is a rough but reliable guide to how long it will take you to double the value of an investment, as long as the interest which accrues to the investment is not withdrawn during that period but is added to the original pot (i.e. compound interest). The rule states:

To find the number of years required to double your money at a given interest rate, you just divide 72 by the interest rate

So if the interest rate was 3 per cent it would take approximately twenty-four years for your money to double while interest at 6 per cent would take twelve years and so on. This doesn't take account of the effect of inflation, which can also be calculated using the rule of 72. So, if inflation averages 3 per cent over the twenty-four-year period, the purchasing power of your pot of money would halve over that time (and if the interest rate also averages 3 per cent then you are back where you started). The investor can only win if, in the long run, interest exceeds inflation. The rule of 72 is notably accurate at percentages below 20 per cent.

It can also apply to things such as population growth, where accurate forecasts are necessary to plan for capacity in everything from housing to health to education. A 1 per cent difference in prediction may not sound much but at 2 per cent growth the need to double capacity will take thirty-six years (72 divided by 2) while at 3 per cent the doubling will occur after only twenty-four years.

The Law of 29

How often do you have to be seduced, cajoled or infuriated by advertisements for a new product before you finally succumb and buy the thing? According to one marketing theory:

Individuals will purchase a new product or service after having been exposed to related advertising 29 times.

The thinking behind the law – and both 'thinking' and 'law' are being used loosely here – is that consumers are generally uninterested or even wary of new products. Only after repeated exposure, whether through traditional advertising, texts, e-mails, product placement, and so on, will they take the risk. The '29' figure is not carved in stone; rather, it translates as 'quite a lot'. Indeed, I suspect that the number was chosen because '25' or '30' would sound like guesswork. The process of sending frequent promotional messages is sometimes known as 'drip marketing'.

The 3–6–3 Rule

This is a 'rule' which looks back to the days when banks were just banks, solid, stolid and dull institutions, rather than the 24/7 marketing machines which they became after regulations were loosened in the 1980s. Originating in the United States but applicable in Britain and elsewhere, the 3–6–3 Rule indicates that bankers should:

> Pay 3 percent interest on deposits, lend money out at 6 percent, and be ready to tee off at the golf course by 3 pm.

After the banking crash and associated financial disasters that began in 2007–8 there was some nostalgia for those unambitious days. As US law professor William Quirk said: 'I would put them [bankers] back on the golf course at three p.m. – where they are not going to be doing that much harm.'

The Pareto Principle

Named for Vilfredo Pareto (1848–1923), a French-born Italian economist and sociologist, the Pareto Principle is also known as the 80–20 rule and the law of the vital few. Early in the twentieth century Pareto noted that 20 per cent of the population owned 80 per cent of the land in Italy, and later observers extended this distribution pattern to other fields. In economics, the Pareto Principle holds that:

20% of invested input is responsible for 80% of the results obtained.

The principle can always be expressed in reverse (e.g. when several factors are in play, 80 per cent of consequences will result from 20 per cent of the causes). It seems to apply in a rule-of-thumb way across the business world, so that 80 per cent of sales are predicted to come from 20 per cent of the clients, while 20 per cent of clients (presumably not the same ones) will be responsible for 80 per cent of the complaints. Or that the efforts of one-fifth of a company's workforce will be responsible for four-fifths of its profits – and a different fifth responsible for most of the company's problems. On an individual level, a relatively small proportion of a person's time at work may result in the most productive part of the outcome. To put it most broadly, the Pareto Principle indicates that there is no neat equivalence between input and output.

The Pizza Principle

A minor and faintly bizarre economic 'law' points to the fact that, in New York, there is a synchronicity between changes in the cost of a slice of pizza and a single ride on the subway. The Pizza Principle, sometimes known as the New York City Pizza Connection, states that:

> Not only is there a rough equivalence in the price of a pizza slice and a subway ride but an increase in the cost of one will shortly be followed by an increase in the other.

The linkage was first observed by Eric Bram, a patent lawyer, writing in the *New York Times* in 1980. He noted that it had obtained for twenty years since 1960, at which time the fare stood 15 cents as did the pizza slice (regular, tomato and mozzarella, no elaborate toppings). The connection has held good for the next thirty and more years, even though there may be minor lags in the system. For example, in 2002, the midtown 'off-the-street' slice was retailing at $2 while the fare remained stuck at $1.50; but within a few months the subway also rose to $2 after eight years without a change. Other synchronous rises have followed at more frequent intervals. Generally, the pizza slice leads the way with the subway cost running behind and therefore the Pizza Principle has a genuine, if somewhat limited, predictive value as an economic law.

3

Arts

Film

Censorship, Hollywood, genre tropes

The Hays Code

The Hays Code was the earliest American attempt to control what people could watch in the cinema. Named after the one-time US postmaster general Will H. Hays, who became head of the Motion Pictures Producers and Distributors Association, the Code was a set of rules which governed scenarios, images, dialogue – everything in fact – permissible in film between the 1930s and the 1960s. Rather like the British system of film censorship, it was enforced not by the US federal government or any individual states but by Hollywood itself because the studios feared government intervention if they didn't keep their own house in order.

The general principles were:

1   No picture shall be produced that will lower the moral standards of those who see it. Hence the sympathy of the audience should never be thrown to the side of crime, wrongdoing, evil or sin.

2   Correct standards of life, subject only to the requirements of drama and entertainment, shall be presented.

3   Law, natural or human, shall not be ridiculed, nor shall sympathy be created for its violation.

Among the particular requirements of the Hays Code were:

- Revenge in modern times shall not be justified.
- The use of firearms should be restricted to the essentials.
- Illegal drug traffic must never be presented.
- Excessive and lustful kissing, lustful embraces, suggestive postures and gestures, are not to be shown.
- Undressing scenes should be avoided, and never used save where essential to the plot.
- Miscegenation (sex relationships between the white and black races) is forbidden.
- Pointed profanity (this includes the words, God, Lord, Jesus, Christ – unless used reverently – Hell, S.O.B. [son of a bitch], damn, Gawd), or every other profane or vulgar expression however used, is forbidden.

- The treatment of bedrooms must be governed by good taste and delicacy.

What is so surprising about the Hays Code is not the content of the rules but that they lasted as long as they did. Their effect started to fade in the 1950s under the impact of television, the example of 'daring' foreign films, and the willingness of directors and film studios to challenge old standards.

For comparison, have a look at the current guidelines laid down by the British Board of Film Classification (BBFC) which until 1984 was known as the BBFC – the same initials and words except that the C stood for Censors. In itself, the switch of words from Censors to Classification is a measure of how far attitudes towards censorship have changed. The intention is not to prevent adults watching what they want to watch, but to grade material so that its suitability for particular ages is made clear. The Board's guiding principles are:

- To protect children and vulnerable adults from potentially harmful or otherwise unsuitable media content.

- To empower consumers, particularly parents and those with responsibility for children, to make informed viewing decisions.

The Board doesn't issue hard-and-fast rules about sex and violence but puts great stress on context, explaining that the intended audience and their expectations must be taken into account, along with the setting of the work (historical, fantasy, realistic, etc.), the style in which it's presented, and even the age of the piece. This explains why some works which were previously cut or banned outright in the 1970s (*Straw Dogs, The Texas Chain Saw Massacre*) can now pass the censors – sorry, classifiers. Just about the only area where it's possible to see hard-and-fast rules operating is when it comes to bad language. Here the BBFC breaks it down by age and grade, and in its mildest categorization includes terms that would have been banned under the US Hays Code:

U – 'Infrequent use only of very mild[1] bad language.'

PG – 'Mild bad language only.'[2]

12A/12 – 'Moderate[3] language is allowed. The use of strong language (for example, "fuck") must be infrequent.'

15 – 'There may be frequent use of strong language (for example, "fuck"). The strongest terms (for example, "cunt") may be acceptable if justified by the context. Aggressive or repeated use of the strongest language is unlikely to be acceptable.'

18 – No constraints on language.

The Bechdel Rule

This originated with the American cartoonist and graphic novelist Alison Bechdel. As far back in 1985, in her comic strip *Dykes to Watch Out For*, she has one female character telling

---

[1] Very mild: damn, hell, God, sod.

[2] Mild: bastard, piss, shit, bollocks, crap, slag, tosser, Jesus, Christ.

[3] Moderate: wanker, prick, bitch.

another that she will only go to a movie if it satisfies three basic requirements. They are:

1   It has to have at least two women in it,

2   who talk to each other,

3   about something besides a man.

Bechdel says now that she is ambivalent about the test/rule which bears her name and explains in an item on her blog (dated 8 November 2013) that she thinks the idea originally came, via a friend, from Virginia Woolf's *A Room of One's Own* where the question is asked: 'Suppose, for instance, that men were only represented in literature as the lovers of women, and were never the friends of men, soldiers, thinkers, dreamers; how few parts in the plays of Shakespeare could be allotted to them: how literature would suffer!'

The Bechdel test, as it's now usually known, has become more prominent at a time when cinema screens are swamped by computer-generated imagery (CGI) blockbusters featuring monsters from the deep, aliens from outer space, or superheroes who, if they happen to be women, are there mostly to show off their cutely armoured breasts and provide back-up for the men. One commentator pointed out that even *Zero Dark Thirty* (2012), directed by Kathryn Bigelow and starring Jessica Chastain as a persistent and heroic Central Intelligence Agency (CIA) operative, still failed the Bechdel test despite having a lead female character and other high-ranking women who actually talk to each other. The reason? It's because the women don't talk about anything except one specific man – Osama Bin Laden.

At least the subject is taken seriously in Sweden where a chain of cinemas has adopted an 'A' rating for films which pass the Bechdel test.

Goldman's Law

William Goldman (b. 1931) is a novelist and Hollywood screen writer responsible for some of the most entertaining and intelligent scripts of what in retrospect looks like a golden period – that is, from the late 1960s until the largely disastrous rise of CGI some thirty years later. Goldman wrote *Butch Cassidy and the Sundance Kid* (1969), *All the President's Men* (1976) and *The Princess Bride* (1987) and much else. In his book *Adventures in the Screen Trade* (1983), a highly entertaining mixture of memoir and how-to-do-it, Goldman says that if there's one thing he's learned in his years in Hollywood it is that:

NOBODY KNOWS ANYTHING.

The point is so important that Goldman capitalizes these three words and repeatedly comes back to the rule throughout the book. NOBODY KNOWS ANYTHING. As an example he cites the reaction of producer Richard Zanuck to the initial preview of the musical *Star!*[4] (1968) which featured Julie Andrews as Gertrude

---

[4] Star! An exclamation mark after a title is like a shot of marshmallow across the bows: a warning that you'd better enjoy yourself, or else. A disproportionate number of film musicals – *Oklahoma!, Oliver!, Hello, Dolly!, Moulin Rouge!, Mamma Mia!* – come backed-up with exclamations, as do some camp film outings with titles such as *Faster, Pussycat! Kill. Kill!, Attack of the Killer Tomatoes!* and *Airplane!*

Lawrence. The preview went so well that Zanuck cancelled any further test showings and wired his famous producer father, Darryl F. to say: 'We're home! Better than Sound of Music.' As Goldman says, 'The Sound of Music was then the most popular movie in history, and Star! went on to become the Edsel[5] of 20th Century Fox.'

Wilder's Rules

Part of the great exodus of talent which emigrated from Europe to the United States as the Nazis rose to power, the Austrian-born film director and screen-writer Billy Wilder (1906–2002) was one of the most distinguished and versatile figures in Hollywood. Wilder was brilliantly adept in a variety of genres from the criminal noir of *Double Indemnity* to the acerbic comedy of *The Apartment* to an unconventional and underrated homage to the great detective in *The Private Life of Sherlock Holmes*. Wilder had a taste for aphorism and once said: 'I have ten commandments. The first nine are, thou shalt not bore. The tenth is, thou shalt have right of final cut.' In a set of interviews with Cameron Crowe, also a writer-director, and published in book form as Conversations with Wilder (1999), the 93-year old director elaborated on his commandments.

---

[5] Named after Edsel B. Ford, the only son of founding father Henry Ford, the Edsel automobile was a famous flop of the 1950s. The Ford Motor Company poured millions of dollars into its development, so confident of success that they failed to carry out any proper marketing research. Had they done so, it might have emerged that the not dissimilar German word Esel means 'donkey'.

These are sometimes seen as rules for writers but they could apply just as well to directors.

1   The audience is fickle.

2   Grab 'em by the throat and never let 'em go.

3   Develop a clean line of action for your leading character.

4   Know where you're going.

5   The more subtle and elegant you are in hiding your plot points, the better you are as a writer.

6   If you have a problem with the third act, the real problem is in the first act.

7   A tip from Lubitsch:[6] Let the audience add up two plus two. They'll love you forever.

8   In doing voice-overs, be careful not to describe what the audience already sees. Add to what they're seeing.

9   The event that occurs at the second act curtain triggers the end of the movie.

10 The third act must build, build, build in tempo and action until the last event, and then – that's it. Don't hang around.

Scream rules

The Scream films make up one of the most successful horror franchises in screen history. Post-modern, arch and self-mocking, the four films are populated by characters who are all too aware

---

[6] German-born Ernst Lubitsch (1892–1947) was, like Billy Wilder, a European émigré to Hollywood. Wilder was one of the co-writers on *Ninotchka*, which starred Greta Garbo and which Lubitsch directed.

that they are participating in a horror scenario. In the original *Scream* (1996), a bunch of teens – and so slasher fodder – are watching a video of *Halloween* (1978), the film credited with kicking off the horror revival of the 1980s and introducing tropes such as the survival of the lone 'good' and virginal girl when everyone around her has been cut to ribbons. Accordingly, one of the Scream teens freeze-frames the Halloween video in order to deliver the following rules:

1 'You can never have sex. (Sex equals death.)'

2 'You can never drink or do drugs. (A sin factor. It's an extension of number one.)'

3 'Never ever, EVER under any circumstances say "I'll be right back" because you won't be back.'

Subsequent Scream films refined and added to the rules, always with an eye to the fact that sequels are expected to be both the same and different. ('The body count is always bigger'; 'The death scenes are always much more elaborate – more blood, more gore'; 'Never, ever, under any circumstances, assume the killer is dead.') By the time of *Scream 4* the cross-references and films-within-films produce two false starts in the first ten minutes alone, and the whole thing threatens to disappear up its own self-referentiality.

Laws of Cartoon Motion

The world of film is sometimes close to real life and sometimes a long way away from it but, unless the story demands superman-style powers, bolstered by a large dose of CGI, the laws of physics are there to be obeyed. The man in the street cannot turn aside and walk through a wall. Characters falling off the edge of a building will continue to fall until something – a car roof, a hotel awning, a road – stops their descent. By contrast, animated-cartoon characters, especially animal ones, have never been subject to earthbound rules. But there are rules nonetheless. In 1980 the writer Mark O'Donnell set out to systematize them in an article for *Esquire* magazine. O'Donnell (1954–2012) had nothing to do with cartoons – he wrote the book for the musical Hairspray – but he had an eye for the logic underpinning their absurdity. These are O'Donnell's Laws of Cartoon Motion:

I: Any body suspended in space will remain in space until made aware of its situation.

(Daffy Duck steps off a cliff, expecting further pastureland. He loiters in midair, soliloquizing flippantly, until he chances to look down. At this point, the familiar principle of 32 feet per second per second takes over.)

II: Any body in motion will tend to remain in motion until solid matter intervenes suddenly.

(Whether shot from a cannon or in hot pursuit on foot, cartoon characters are so absolute in their momentum that only a telephone pole or an outsize boulder retards their forward motion absolutely.)

III: Any body passing through solid matter will leave a perforation conforming to its perimeter.

(Also called the silhouette of passage, this phenomenon is the speciality of victims of directed-pressure explosions and of reckless cowards who are so eager

to escape that they exit directly through the wall of a
house, leaving a cookie-cutout-perfect hole.)

IV: The time required for an object to fall twenty stories is
greater than or equal to the time it takes for whoever
knocked it off the ledge to spiral down twenty flights to
attempt to capture it unbroken.

V: All principles of gravity are negated by fear.

(Psychic forces are sufficient in most bodies for a shock
to propel them directly away from the earth's surface.
A spooky noise or an adversary's signature sound
will induce motion upward, usually to the cradle of a
chandelier, a treetop, or the crest of a flagpole.)

VI: As speed increases, objects can be in several places at once.

(This is particularly true of tooth-and-claw fights, in
which a character's head may be glimpsed emerging
from the cloud of altercation at several places
simultaneously. This effect is common as well among
bodies that are spinning or being throttled.)

VII: Certain bodies can pass through solid walls painted to
resemble tunnel entrances; others cannot.

(This trompe l'oeil inconsistency has baffled generations,
but at least it is known that whoever paints an entrance
on a wall's surface to trick an opponent will be unable
to pursue him into this theoretical space. The painter
is flattened against the wall when he attempts to follow
into the painting.)

VIII: Any violent rearrangement of feline matter is impermanent.

(Cartoon cats possess even more deaths than the traditional nine lives might comfortably afford. They can be decimated, spliced, splayed, accordion-pleated, spindled, or disassembled, but they cannot be destroyed. After a few moments of blinking self pity, they reinflate, elongate, snap back, or solidify. Corollary: A cat will assume the shape of its container.)

IX: Everything falls faster than an anvil.

X: For every vengeance there is an equal and opposite revengeance.

Laws of crime films

Of course there are laws and conventions for non-animated films and TV narratives too. In fact, the widespread use of CGI makes it difficult sometimes to distinguish between an animated film and a live-action one. Below are a few of the rules or tropes which have been appearing in crime films for a long time now. In tribute to Mark O'Donnell there are ten of them – call them Gooden's laws if you like.

I: Any escaping murderer/thief/bad guy or gang will, when putting on the radio in their getaway car or switching on the TV news in their fleapit motel, see and hear a report of the very crime which they have just committed. The report will appear either straightaway or after minimal channel-hopping.

II: Any character who finds herself – and it's almost always a woman – in a place which is too wild or inaccessible for mobile/cellphone coverage early in the story will, before the end, be pursued to that same spot or have to communicate vital information from it or both.[7] If, by good fortune, there is a signal, it will be weak and patchy and, in any case, the phone battery will be running very low.

III: The arrival of a mysterious e-mail in the detective's in-box is never spam but either a riddling tip-off about a crime or a direct (but also taunting) communication from the perpetrator.

IV: A related rule to III in film means that, when the detective receives a phone call from the serial killer, it always occurs in a crowded office/squad room, which has to be hushed with frantic arm gestures.

V: Another related rule of long-distance communication: attempts to trace the call to the detective almost always fail because the savvy killer breaks the connection too soon, although the general area from which the call has been made can sometimes be located. In the unlikely event that the exact spot is pinpointed, the caller will have got away just before the police arrive.

---

[7] The rule about mobile phones and blind spots is related to a dramatic principle sometimes known as Chekhov's gun. The Russian playwright observed: 'One must not put a loaded rifle on the stage if no one is thinking of firing it.' A similar moment occurs on screen when a desk drawer is opened to retrieve something innocuous (papers, a cigarette case), and a gun is revealed at the same time. The audience knows the gun will be used later on. Similarly, the audience knows that the mobile phone/blind-spot situation will be exploited at some point.

(In pre-mobile days this was sometimes indicated by a phone handset dangling in a call-box.)

VI: The appearance of a cat/mouse/trapped bird which spooks a character wandering round an empty house in the dark – and which also spooks the audience – will shortly be followed by the appearance of something or someone genuinely frightening.

VII: Two policemen are unable to meet in a corridor/foyer/communal space in a police station without having a public argument and sometimes (almost) coming to blows. This tends to apply only if there is a significant difference in rank, as between a maverick detective and his/her by-the-book boss.

VIII: Any individual arrested early in the story on suspicion of having committed the major crime did not do it, although allowance must be made for the occasional double bluff.

IX: The room/lair of the serial killer/terrorist mastermind will be plastered with newspaper cuttings/illicit snaps of victims/street plans/connecting arrows and so on, whose arrangement and obsessiveness provide an eerie echo of the same set-up on the pin-board in the police station.

X: In a Poirot-style round-up of characters at the climax of a whodunnit the one face the camera will not linger on, until the very end, is that of the murderer.

Press

Rules of journalism

These humorous rules were formulated in 2007 by Michael Rosenberg, a sports journalist with the Detroit Free Press. There were originally nine of them and several have a specifically US application. Others, however, don't, and anybody who spends more than a moment in the company of the great British press will see their relevance.

Afflict the comfortable and comfort the afflicted. Then, after the afflicted become comfortable, afflict them again. This should provide an endless supply of news stories.

Be balanced. No matter what anybody says, find somebody to say the opposite. If a scientist claims to have a cure for cancer, find somebody who says cancer does not exist.

When deciding which tragedies deserve the most prominent coverage, use this simple math: 10,000 foreigners = one cute white American chick.

Betteridge's Law of Headlines

Ian Betteridge is a British tech writer who in 2009 on his Technovia website came up with the following maxim:

Any headline which ends in a question mark can be answered by the word no.

The political commentator, John Rentoul, in his Eagle Eye blog for the *Independent* has long collected examples of 'Questions To Which The Answer Is No'; his QTWTAIN no.1,000 was the cover headline on *Time* magazine which asked: 'Can Google Solve Death?' Others include 'Was the downfall of Richard III caused by a strawberry?' and 'Could climate change turn humans into hobbits?'

The originator of the law, Ian Betteridge, has an explanation for the headline which ends with a question mark: 'The reason why journalists use that style of headline is that they know the story is probably bullshit, and don't actually have the sources and facts to back it up, but still want to run it.'

An earlier and slightly mysterious version of Betteridge's law applies to the rarefied world of particle physics. Hinchliffe's Rule – the mystery lies in who Hinchliffe is or was – states that any scientific paper or website posting whose title ends with a question mark is to be answered with a 'no' or, at best, 'probably not'. A recent example would be the 'Neutrinos faster than light?' sensation story of 2011 in which experiments appeared to show, briefly and erroneously, that there was something in the universe which could travel faster than light. But the question mark after the suggestion really indicated that the answer was already known and that it was 'no'. There is even a spoof paper available online, apparently written by one Boris Peon (*sic*), and titled 'Is Hinchliffe's Rule True?'. It consists of nothing more than a title page with this abstract or summary: 'Hinchliffe has asserted that whenever the title of a paper is a question with a yes/no answer, the answer is always no. This paper demonstrates that Hinchliffe's assertion is false, but only if it is true.'

A related observation to do with veracity and the use of punctuation marks has sometimes been called the Law of Exclamation. Deriving from the Internet, it states that:

> The more exclamation points used in an email (or other posting), the more likely it is a complete lie. This is also true for excessive capital letters.

Crossword rules

Many guides have been written on how to solve crosswords, especially the cryptic variety which are a favourite with the British. Clues in 'cryptics' consist of a definition of the answer but also a riddling element, involving anagrams or other forms of word-play, often misleading by intention (e.g. 'flower' might signify a river while 'a wicked object' could point to a candle). There are a host of rules which govern the construction of the grid and the styling of the clues, all of which constrain the setters as they tread the line between baffling the solver and playing fair. But there are also rules indicating what kinds of words are not allowed as answers, at least in the *Times*, which has arguably the best crossword out of the ones which appear everyday in the papers. In a *Times* crossword you must have:

1 No living people.[8]

2 No brand names.

---

[8] Although references to the queen are allowed (mostly because the ER abbreviation is too useful to pass up as part of the cryptic cluing).

3   No rude words.[9]

4   No names of serious diseases.[10]

Language, style and substance

The Pooh Pooh Theory and others

One of the most impressive and enduring achievements of the
nineteenth century was the great project which became the
Oxford English Dictionary. Like other great projects, it overran
its original schedule and far exceeded its expected costs (the first
volume covering A-Ant appeared in 1884, but the whole thing
would not be completed until 1928). The period leading up to
the Victorian era saw a new interest not merely in the English
language but in the origins of language itself as a faculty which
is unique to humans. It was a matter of tracing out connections
and digging for roots. How did we learn to speak? How did we
form words?

---

[9] Other papers have a more liberal approach. *The Guardian* sometimes has suggestive
clues and risqué answers. *The Private Eye* crossword is famous for them. (Sample clue:
A minute implant in boob operation, which grows quickly; Answer: BAMBOO –
anagram of BOOB+A+M[inute].)

[10] John Graham, a witty and inventive crossword setter in the *Guardian* where he was
known as Araucaria (=monkey puzzle tree), announced his diagnosis of cancer of the
oesophagus with a puzzle which included clues for those words as well as others such
as Macmillan, nurse, stent, endoscopy and sunset. That puzzle appeared in January
2013 to the general admiration of the crossword community; John Graham died in
November of that year, aged 92, but continued compiling puzzles until the end.

A variety of theories emerged in the attempt to explain the origins of language. To later generations these sound distinctly odd, if only because of the names which they were given, in some cases as a sign of mockery. For example, there was the Pooh-Pooh or Interjectional Theory which maintained that:

> People started to speak by emitting instinctive sounds, stimulated by pain, anger, fear, frustration or something similar.

While the bow-wow theory held that:

> Humans started speaking in onomatopoeic imitation of the noises made by animals or natural phenomena like thunderstorms or the noise of the sea.

The flaws in these theories are much greater than any plausible elements they may contain. Regarding the pooh-pooh one: involuntary or semi-involuntary utterances such as a cry of pain or a gasp of surprise or a tut-tutting sound are relatively small in number and have little connection to the sounds of vowels and consonants in real words. As for the bow-wow theory: there are not many onomatopoeic words in any language and the older ones, which are inevitably those connected to animal noises, tend to be different in different tongues (to English ears a pig goes 'oink, oink' while to Russian ones it is rendered as 'khryoo, khryoo'). Although imitation does play a part in language development, for the bow-wow theory to hold there would have to be greater similarities between various onomatopoeic terms across different languages.

Then there is the ding-dong theory. Nothing to do with Leslie Phillips and his 'I say' catchphrase, ding-dong applies to what one nineteenth-century linguistic scholar termed 'symphonesis', a kind of agreement or reaction between what is happening in the external world and lip-and-tongue movements. So, as the mother's breast approaches the baby's mouth, the sound of 'mama' will emerge spontaneously because of the movement of the child's lips. If the ding-dong theory sounds fanciful, then that is because it is. And there is no space to comment at length on the Yo-He-Ho Theory (language arose out of the communal grunts uttered by our primitive ancestors as they worked together) or the La-La Theory (language arose out of our ancestors' desire for love, their wish to play and what specialists describe as 'other socio-affective states').

Five rules of grammar and usage . . .
. . . which you do not need to keep

The battle for a form of the English language which is good or correct (not always the same thing) is an odd conflict, because it is fought hard on one side while the other side responds by doing almost nothing. Yet, inexorably and over a length of time, it is this indolent side which is winning. The warriors are those lined up in the correct camp who maintain that there are clear rules about grammar and usage which have to be observed and enforced. They are the prescriptivists. The more ragged band on the other side are often described as 'descriptivist' because they simply note that language is changing, and that the majority usage will eventually win out, whether it is formally 'correct' or not. As an example of the gap between the two, a linguistic pedant would object to my use of 'are' in the previous sentence in tandem with the noun 'band', since one is singular and the other plural, but the plain fact is that few people would notice and fewer still would care. And this is why the prescriptivists are destined to lose to the descriptivists.

Yes, there are rules of language but the most important of them are embedded and absorbed early on, without any conscious process of learning. Which English speaker can remember the discovery that adjectives are put in front of nouns (unlike in French) or that the verb rarely comes at the end of the sentence (unlike in German)? Most of the other so-called rules about the English language – almost always in its spoken form and often when written down – are just frills. And quite a few of them don't need to be observed at all. So here are five principal rules which are to be broken as necessary, with brief, bracketed explanations attached.

1   You should not start a sentence with conjunctions such as 'and' or 'but'.

    (A string of sentences starting with conjunctions becomes predictable and so is better avoided. But there is no reason why a conjunctive start shouldn't be used occasionally, especially when you want to throw emphasis on the beginning of a sentence or to produce a terse or breathless effect, something frequently deployed in journalism, advertising copy and thrillers, and often found without a verb. As here. And here.)

2   You should not end a sentence with a preposition.

(Prepositions put at the end of sentences are sometimes referred to as 'stranded', and if a large distance separates the preposition and its reference point then the resulting sentence can feel somewhat strung-out. 'There were people in every department he hadn't yet got round to having a word with' is fine when spoken though a bit cumbersome if written down. But most of the time, and if it sounds natural, the preposition can comfortably go at the end.)

3   You should never split an infinitive.

(The most famous exception to this silly non-rule is the Star Trek mission-statement 'to boldly go where no man has gone before', where changing the position of the adverbial 'boldly' – to go boldly – would change the rhythm of the phrase, and not for the better. If you don't even notice whether an infinitive has been split or not, then you are on the side of the angels.)

4   You should observe the difference between 'who' and 'whom'.

('Who' will almost always do. Agitating about whether it should be 'who' or 'whom' often causes people to mistakenly use the second, as in 'The person whom the police believe committed the crime has left the country.' From the pedantic point of view, you are more likely to be pulled up over this than a statement like 'He's someone who I'm never going to speak to again', which is just as incorrect. It may be that 'whom' sticks out in a sentence, especially when spoken aloud, because it signals that the user is striving to be correct while the much more familiar form of 'who' goes unremarked.)

5 And the difference between 'less' and 'fewer'.

('Less' is supposed to qualify what are called mass nouns while 'fewer' qualifies count nouns, so that one talks about 'less sand' and 'fewer stones', or 'less cheese' (of a single block of Cheddar) and 'fewer cheeses' (of the selection on a counter). But in practice 'less' will fit almost all cases.)

Hartman's Law of Prescriptivist Retaliation

Jed Hartman wasn't the first to come up with this law but he formulated it neatly and, perhaps more important, he gave it an impressive title. The term 'Prescriptivist' in this context refers to those who attempt to lay down firm rules for language use (see previous entry).

Hartman's Law of Prescriptivist Retaliation reads:

Any article or statement about correct grammar, punctuation, or spelling is bound to contain at least one error.[11]

---

[11] Both Hartman's and McKean's Laws contain an example of the American serial comma, that is, the insertion of a comma before a conjunction and the final term in a list: '. . . correct grammar, punctuation, or spelling' and '. . . at least one grammatical, spelling, or typographical error'. This is not so usual in British English and would be removed by most copy-editors. Which all goes to show that 'correctness' is, at least in part, a question of culture and practice, or as it would be spelt in the US 'practise'. And 'spelt' is usually spelt 'spelled' over there too.

A slight variation was formulated around the same time by American lexicographer Erin McKean. Her law states:

> Any correction of the speech or writing of others will contain at least one grammatical, spelling, or typographical error.

An earlier and more lengthy version was codified in 1982 by John Bangsund of the Victorian Society of Editors in Australia. Bangsund was responsible for the brilliant linguistic coinage of Muphry's Law which describes the process whereby, if you set out to highlight others' written mistakes, you will make your own blunders. Conversely, if you thank people for help, that merely increases the likelihood of errors for which they are accountable. It is important not to confuse Muphry's Law with Murphy's Law (see entry). In full, Muphry's Law dictates that:

(a) if you write anything criticizing editing or proofreading, there will be a fault of some kind in what you have written;

(b) if an author thanks you in a book for your editing or proofreading, there will be mistakes in the book;

(c) the stronger the sentiment expressed in (a) and (b), the greater the fault;

(d) any book devoted to editing or style will be internally inconsistent.

These related laws[12] are informed by the spirit of schadenfreude. We enjoy seeing pedants and prescriptivists getting their

---

[12] There is also Skitt's Law, which tends refer to the Internet (Any post correcting an error in another post will contain at least one error itself), and the self-explanatory Iron Law of Nitpicking.

comeuppance (unless we happen to be pedants and prescriptivists ourselves). Hence the reference to retaliation in Hartman's Law. Examples of Hartman's/McKean's/Muphry's Law are not hard to come by. When Lynne Truss's super-selling guide *Eats, Shoots & Leaves: The Zero Tolerance Approach to Punctuation* appeared in the United States, it prompted a highly critical review in *The New Yorker* magazine which speculated that the whole book might be a 'hoax' and which began: 'The first punctuation mistake [. . .] appears in the dedication, where a nonrestrictive clause is not preceded by a comma.' When the *Sun* attacked Prime Minister Gordon Brown in 2009 for misspelling a soldier's surname in a letter of condolence to his mother, the newspaper got the surname wrong on its website. And when, in the summer of 2013, the then education secretary Michael Gove wrote a memo to his staff about writing good, clear English, he included the familiar injunction: 'Use the active, not the passive voice.' It was quickly pointed out that he had used a passive construction in the very first sentence of his own memo.

Considine's Law

A law relating to the ones above about typos, misprints and other slips, and named for the US reporter and writer Bob Considine states that:

> If a single word or letter can change the entire meaning of a sentence, the probability of an error being made will be in direct proportion to the embarrassment it will cause.

Considine's Law is accurate enough but he might have added that the more the embarrassment caused to the perpetrator of the mistake, the greater the amusement for the reader. The satirical magazine *Private Eye* specializes in reproducing slips such as those which substitute 'pubic' for 'public' or 'sex' for 'six' in print, while a notable example of Considine's Law occurred in the online edition of the *Daily Telegraph* in March 2010 when a breakthrough at the European Organisation for Nuclear Research (CERN) in Geneva was headlined as follows: 'Large Hardon Collider breaks energy record.' The paper moved almost as fast as all those sub-atomic particles whizzing round the Large Hadron Collider to correct the error.

Rule of three

Like several other numbers (5, 7, 9) the number three possesses – or is supposed to possess – particular powers, and to have an attraction, glamour or even authority which somehow makes it superior to other numbers. Certainly, when it comes to titles, speech-making, copy-writing, slogan-making and communication in general the rule is that:

> Concepts or ideas put forward as a threesome are inherently more attractive, satisfying and memorable than formulations made in different quantities.

That three is an ideal number is a notion that it is easier to illustrate than to analyse, and the story begins in fairy-tale, legend and popular literature. There are *Three Little Pigs* and *Three Billy Goats Gruff*, *Three Wise Men* and *Three Blind Mice*, *Three Musketeers*

and *Three Men in a Boat*. The story of 'Goldilocks and the Three
Bears' is built on groups of three (bears, bowls of porridge, chairs,
beds), and the idea that only one out of the three is 'just right'
has led to the Goldilocks narrative being used in both economics
and astronomy to describe an optimal situation, for example for
the development of life on another planet. Moving away from
nursery stories, the title of Graham Greene's film and novel *The
Third Man* was widely applied to Kim Philby, the double agent
who defected to the Soviet Union in 1963 in the wake of his two
fellow traitors Guy Burgess and Donald Maclean. Then there
are the three witches in Shakespeare's *Macbeth* while in *The
Merchant of Venice* the three suitors of the beautiful Portia are
required, under the terms of her father's will, to choose between
three caskets of gold, silver and lead, only one of which contains
the 'right' answer. (In accordance with another rule of narrative
surprise it is in the lead casket.) In Dickens's *A Christmas Carol*,
the miser Ebenezer Scrooge is visited by a triad of spirits, the
Ghost of Christmas Past, the Ghost of Christmas Present and the
Ghost of Christmas Yet to Come.

The rule of three often applies to jokes whether in their
subject matter – 'An Englishman, Irishman and Scotsman . . . '/'A
priest, a minister and a rabbi . . .' – or in their structure, so that
the same concept is repeated with variations, the first time to
establish context, the second to confirm the pattern and increase
expectation, and the third to provide the punchline.[13] A similar

---

[13] As in this gag from an old TV comedy when the speaker says to someone with hair
problems : 'Can I get you anything? Cup of coffee? Doughnut? Toupee?'

tripartite structure can be seen in dozens of phrases such as 'Tom, Dick and Harry', 'Rag, Tag and Bobtail', 'Lock, Stock and Barrel', 'beginning, middle and end', 'Snap, Crackle and Pop', the legal firm which features in *Private Eye* as 'Sue, Grabbit and Runne' and even the simple letters 'X, Y and Z'. Leaders and nations frequently brandish the three-part slogan, often in a jingoistic or bellicose spirit, from Julius Caesar's apocryphal use of 'Veni, vidi, vici' ('I came, I saw, I conquered') to the Nazis 'Ein Volk, ein Reich, ein Führer' ('One People, One Empire, One Leader') or Fascist Italy's 'Credere, obbedire, combattere' ('Believe, obey, fight') or the Vichy French slogan 'Travail, famille, patrie' ('Work, family, fatherland'). On a more elevated level the US Constitution promises 'Life, liberty and the pursuit of happiness' while many will remember Tony Blair's proclamation that his priorities were 'Education, education, education', a triple iteration perhaps suggested by the estate agents' mantra of 'location, location, location'.

Within stories, too, especially if they involve quests, riddles or puzzles, the same pattern of three may be observed. The genie from the magic lamp grants three wishes, as does possession of a monkey's paw in the horror story of the same name by W. W. Jacobs. On screen it is often the third key on the bunch which opens the lock, or the third attempt which finds the right combination to the safe or the correct password for accessing vital information. After a couple of misguided attempts it will be the third path which leads to the cave/dragon/treasure. There are good narrative reasons for this: success at the first attempt would be too lucky or easy while failure at the second attempt raises suspense and anxiety. But to stretch out the process beyond three to four or more attempts also stretches the patience of the audience. Apart from all this, there seems to be something psychologically and emotionally satisfying in the rule of three, its pattern and rhythm. First this, then this, then that.

Books

Reading . . .

Page 99 Rule

The following rule or test is supposed to have been put forward by Ford Madox Ford (1873–1939), the author of *The Good Soldier* and *Parade's End*:

> Open the book to page ninety-nine and read, and the quality of the whole will be revealed to you.

This quotation may be correct as it stands, since it has been repeated often enough with the attribution to Ford Madox Ford. On the other hand, Alexander Theroux, in his introduction to the last book which Ford wrote, a history titled *The March of Literature* (1938), says that the author believed that a passage of good prose was a work of art in itself, independent of context, and that 'he had the habit by way of testing it of always turning to page 90 of an author's work and quoting the first paragraph.'

So which page is the key one: 90 or 99? If one had to pick between the two page reference tests – and, of course Ford might have come up with both of them – then I would plump for the second, the page 90 one. Somehow it sounds more serious, more writerly, and Ford Madox Ford was both of those things. Yet if you want to sample a book in order to decide whether to read it at all, then going for a section between pages 90 and 99 makes sense. Any fireworks from the opening will have long died down, the foundations of the story will be there but the narrative won't be at its point of greatest complexity, let alone near to a denouement. It's like the section of a journey when your time of departure seems quite a while ago while the moment of arrival is still several hours ahead. So if a writer can capture and keep your attention for the routine, workaday stretch that is likely to occur between pages 90 and 99 then the book as a whole may work for you.

Marshall McLuhan (1911–80), the Canadian academic once hailed as the most important thinker since Darwin or Freud and the originator of the Global Village concept, also had his own version of page 99 rule/test except that in his case it was page 69. The choice of number, enough to take the reader well into a book, was not arbitrary. McLuhan believed that the number 3 and numbers divisible by it were lucky for him. The faculty house in Toronto where he took seminars was numbered 39A; his groundbreaking book, *Understanding Media* (1964), which popularized his belief that the 'medium is the message', was split into thirty-three chapters. Presumably McLuhan hadn't heard of the page 90/99 rule, which would have fitted his obsession with threes just as well or better.

A not dissimilar sampling rule for films was suggested in a *New Yorker* magazine article by film critic and commentator,

Richard Brody. Under the heading 'A Great Film Reveals Itself in Five Minutes', Brody suggested taking a DVD of any classic film – *Citizen Kane, Tokyo Story* and *Vertigo* are among the examples he gives – and fast-forwarding to a random point and watching five minutes of it. The experience won't show or tell you everything, he says, but it will be enough to 'arouse admiration, astonishment, and love, as well as the hunger to see the whole movie.'

The five laws of library science

These were the brainchild of Shiyali Ramamrita Ranganathan (1892–1972), a mathematician, theorist and librarian in India who in 1931, while at Madras University, developed the philosophy and practice which should underlie the modern library. His five laws are:

1   Books are for use.
2   Every reader his [or her] book.
3   Every book its reader.
4   Save the time of the reader.
5   The library is a growing organism.

The slightly Zen-like nature of some of these perhaps requires a note of explanation:

1   Books are for use means that a library does not exist to preserve books or keep them metaphorically chained up, as they were literally chained in a medieval monastery,

but to make them freely available to the reader. The first law extends to questions like the siting of libraries and their opening hours so that accessibility and use are maximized.

2   Every reader his [or her] book implies that readers have different interests which will be satisfied by different books. Users have a right to information of all kinds, and part of the librarian's role is to fight against censorship as well as to ensure access for all, without judging people's preferences.

3   Every book its reader suggests that people may need to be brought together with material they require. They may not know exactly what they want, or even that they want it at all, and therefore libraries and librarians have the job of advising, of putting books into their hands and so on. Reference work traditionally falls under this third law.

4   Save the time of the reader by enabling them to find what they want quickly, whether in the stacks or online – helped by the skill of librarians.

5   That the library is a growing organism may sound a rather forlorn maxim in a period of cutbacks and false economies, but the principle is that libraries must adapt and grow with the times to broaden their appeal, to find new custom, enhance their services and so on.

S. R. Ranganathan ('Classification truly charmed me' he once wrote) also developed a system called Colon Classification, so called because of the use of the colon (:). It is a method of cataloguing academic and other publications by breaking down their subject-matter under different headings, beginning with the most general aspect (e.g. medicine) and ending with the most specific (e.g. the date the research was carried out). Ranganathan described how the idea came to him in London while he was watching a salesman demonstrate the versatility of Meccano in Selfridge's. After studying at the School of Librarianship (part of University College, London), Ranganathan returned by boat to India where he put his theories to the test.

> In June 1925, I was sailing back to Madras in the ship M.V. Dumana. The first few days of the voyage were spent in trying out CC [Colon Classification] in its incipient form in classifying the few hundreds of books of the ship's library. This was done as a pilot project. The Captain of the Ship was very friendly and gave me the freedom to arrange and rearrange the books as I liked. Some of the passengers appreciated the helpfulness of the resulting sequence.

. . . and writing

Writers' rules

Most writers enjoy dispensing advice on everything from the right implement (Hemingway preferred using a pencil) to the right subject-matter ('Write what you know' Mark Twain is supposed to have said). But not many writers have actually laid down rules, 10-commandment style. Interestingly, of the various sets given here, the majority are provided by genre writers, reflecting the fact that science-fiction, thrillers and whodunnits are more likely to be formulaic, even rule-bound. Also, it might be observed that these rules are overwhelmingly negative in that they prescribe not what to do but what not to do.

George Orwell's rules

Novelist and essayist George Orwell (1903–50) is famous for his clear, vigorous English. This was more than a question of taste or style. Anyone reading his attacks on political or military euphemisms, or his satirical presentation of doublethink and newspeak in *Nineteen Eighty-Four* (1949), soon understands that for Orwell the use of language was a moral question. These particular rules for writing appeared in his essay 'Politics and the English Language', first published in 1946:

1   Never use a metaphor, simile or other figure of speech which you are used to seeing in print.

2   Never use a long word where a short one will do.

3   If it is possible to cut a word out, always cut it out.

4   Never use the passive where you can use the active.

5   Never use a foreign phrase, a scientific word or a jargon word if you can think of an everyday English equivalent.

6   Break any of these rules sooner than say anything barbarous.

Although George Orwell came up with these rules more than half a century ago, you still find them quoted, and quoted with respect. The only one that raises eyebrows – cliche alert – is the first, in which Orwell warns against the use of cliche. To make his point in the original essay, he picked examples from what he calls 'a huge dump of worn-out metaphors', including '*grist to the mill, fishing in troubled waters, Achilles' heel, swan song, hotbed*.' According to Orwell, such expressions 'have lost all evocative power and are merely used because they save people the trouble of inventing phrases for themselves'. Yet the equivalents for, say, Achilles' heel – vulnerable spot? chink in the armour? – will rarely do the job as effectively or as economically as the original phrase. And attempts to follow Orwell's advice and invent a new metaphor altogether for Achilles' heel – the loosest brick in the wall? a paper link in an iron chain? – are more likely to baffle than enlighten. As Terry Pratchett has said: 'The reason that cliches become cliches is that they are the hammers and screwdrivers in the toolbox of communication.'

Elmore Leonard's rules

Like other US writers such as Kurt Vonnegut and Joseph Heller, Elmore Leonard (1925–2013) started by writing advertising copy. His earliest books were westerns and it was not until the early 1970s that Leonard turned his full attention to the crime novels for which he became famous. His characters tend towards the low-life or the comic, or both, and his dialogue jumps off the page. Above all, nothing he wrote feels strained or literary –

which, in itself, is a literary effect. In 2001 he wrote an article for the *New York Times*, summarizing his approach. He added a paragraph in explanation of each rule but here they are, in brief:

1   Never open a book with weather.

2   Avoid prologues.

3   Never use a verb other than 'said' to carry dialogue.

4   Never use an adverb to modify the verb 'said'.

5   Keep your exclamation points under control.

6   Never use the words 'suddenly' or 'all hell broke loose'.

7   Use regional dialect, patois, sparingly.

8   Avoid detailed descriptions of characters.

9   Don't go into great detail describing places and things.

10   Try to leave out the part that readers tend to skip.

My most important rule is one that sums up the 10.

If it sounds like writing, I rewrite it.

(See also Elmore Leonard's/Ryan's Rules on Armed Robbery in Physical.)

Raymond Chandler's rules

Raymond Chandler (1888–1957) was one of the most important and influential detective writers of the twentieth century. He gave the mystery genre, and specifically the private-eye story, a respectability and literary kudos which it never came near to achieving in its pulp-magazine days. Chandler always had high-profile admirers in Britain who regarded him as more than just a crime writer. So it may be ironic that Chandler, along with slightly earlier writers such as Dashiell Hammett (*The Maltese Falcon*) and James M Cain (*The Postman Always Rings Twice*), was set on turning his back on what he saw as the sterile, contrived puzzles of golden-age detective writing, exactly the kind of story in which the English had always excelled. Chandler had plenty to say about his chosen genre, and it is worth reading, especially his essay 'The Simple Art of Murder' (1950) in which he describes how hard-boiled writers such as Hammett 'took murder out of the Venetian vase and dropped it into the alley'.

His 'Twelve Notes on the Mystery Story' were not published in his lifetime and appear in their usual form below, reduced to ten. The full version, together with extensive notes by Chandler, can be found on various sites including the Golden Age of Detection Wiki, an invaluable resource for anyone interested in classic and out-of-the-way crime writing in its heyday between the two world wars.

1 It [the mystery story] must be credibly motivated, both as to the original situation and the dénouement.

2 It must be technically sound as to the methods of murder and detection.

3 It must be realistic in character, setting and atmosphere. It must be about real people in a real world.

4 It must have a sound story value apart from the mystery element; that is, the investigation itself must be an adventure worth reading.

5   It must have enough essential simplicity to be explained easily when the time comes.

6   It must baffle a reasonably intelligent reader.

7   The solution must seem inevitable once revealed.

8   It must not try to do everything at once. If it is a puzzle story operating in a rather cool, reasonable atmosphere, it cannot also be a violent adventure or a passionate romance.

9   It must punish the criminal in one way or another, not necessarily by operation of the law . . . If the detective fails to resolve the consequences of the crime, the story is an unresolved chord and leaves irritation behind it.

10 It must be honest with the reader.

Chandler didn't always follow his own rules, particularly numbers 5–7, and his novels are a very long way from 'essentially simple'. When the screenwriters on the film version of *The Big Sleep* (1946) got tangled up in the web of motivation, the film's director Howard Hawks sent Chandler a telegram asking who murdered the character of the chauffeur. Chandler's cabled reply was: 'No idea.'

Ronald Knox's rules

If you were looking for the polar opposite to Raymond Chandler or Elmore Leonard in crime writing, then you would be hard put to find a more suitable candidate than Ronald Knox, or Monsignor Ronald Knox as he was sometimes known.

The son of an Anglican bishop and educated at Eton, Knox (1888–1957) was a Catholic convert and priest. And a writer of detective stories. His are archetypal 'golden age' mysteries, and they come equipped with maps and time-tables for checking alibis. Elaborate, artificial, slightly tongue-in-cheek, Knox's work was meant to be enjoyed by bishops, dons and cabinet ministers as they relaxed in their book-lined studies at the end of another day running the world. In 1929 Knox created these ten commandments for the Detection Club, of which he was a founding member (others included Agatha Christie and Dorothy Sayers). Unlike Orwell's and Leonard's rules of style, Knox's are more to do with playing fair by the reader.

1 The criminal must be someone mentioned in the early part of the story, but must not be anyone whose thoughts the reader has been allowed to follow.

2 All supernatural or preternatural agencies are ruled out as a matter of course.

3 Not more than one secret room or passage is allowable.

4 No hitherto undiscovered poisons may be used, nor any appliance which will need a long scientific explanation at the end.

5 No Chinaman must figure in the story.

6 No accident must ever help the detective, nor must he ever have an unaccountable intuition which proves to be right.

7 The detective must not himself commit the crime.

8   The detective must not light on any clues which are not instantly produced for the inspection of the reader.

9   The stupid friend of the detective, the Watson, must not conceal any thoughts which pass through his mind; his intelligence must be slightly, but very slightly, below that of the average reader.

10 Twin brothers, and doubles generally, must not appear unless we have been duly prepared for them.

Dr Fell's ghost-story rules

Dr Gideon Fell was the detective creation of John Dickson Carr (1906–77), the doyen of the locked-room mystery. A portly, opinionated, cape-wearing sleuth, Fell was supposedly modelled on G. K. Chesterton, himself the creator of the priest-detective Father Brown. Out of a large number of Carr's mysteries, *The Hollow Man* (1935) is regularly cited as the best for the ingenuity of its plot and for a famous chapter titled 'The Locked-Room Lecture' in which Dr Fell enumerates the various tricks used by murderers (and locked-room-mystery writers). All very postmodern, especially when the doctor remarks in the course of his lecture that he and the people he's talking to are characters 'in a detective story, and we don't fool the reader by pretending we're not.'

But Dr Fell has views on much else, including the rules required to create a fictional ghost. In response to a comment that a ghost in a story doesn't have to be threatening, he explains:

I will give you the rules, sir. The ghost should be malignant. It should never speak. It should never be transparent but solid.

It should never hold the stage for long, but appear in brief vivid flashes like the poking of a face round a corner. It should never appear in too much light. It should have an old, an academic or ecclesiastical background; a flavour of cloisters or Latin manuscripts.

Kurt Vonnegut's rules

Kurt Vonnegut (1922–2007) had his first big success with *Slaughterhouse-Five* (1969), a novel based partly on his experience as an American prisoner of war in Dresden when it was firebombed by the allies, resulting in 135,000 deaths. Vonnegut survived because he and other prisoners were confined underground in the meat locker of a slaughterhouse. In the 1950s he wrote advertising copy and a couple of neglected novels before he began teaching creative writing at City College in New York, where Joseph Heller – author of another World War II classic *Catch-22* – also taught. Heller told Vonnegut that if it hadn't been for the war, he would have been in the dry-cleaning business; for his part, Vonnegut said he would have been garden editor of the *Indianapolis Star*. Many years later, after fame struck, and in the introduction to a collection of short stories, Vonnegut returned to teacherly mode and listed eight rules for the writing of short stories. They are:

1   Use the time of a total stranger in such a way that he or she will not feel the time was wasted.

2   Give the reader at least one character he or she can root for.

3 Every character should want something, even if it is only a glass of water.

4 Every sentence must do one of two things – reveal character or advance the action.

5 Start as close to the end as possible.

6 Be a sadist. No matter how sweet and innocent your leading characters, make awful things happen to them – in order that the reader may see what they are made of.

7 Write to please just one person. If you open a window and make love to the world, so to speak, your story will get pneumonia.

8 Give your readers as much information as possible as soon as possible. To hell with suspense. Readers should have such complete understanding of what is going on, where and why, that they could finish the story themselves, should cockroaches eat the last few pages.

And in a final book of essays, *A Man without a Country* (2005), Kurt Vonnegut came up with another characteristically grouchy and perverse piece of stylistic advice to writers:

Here is a lesson in creative writing. First rule: Do not use semicolons. They are transvestite hermaphrodites representing absolutely nothing. All they do is show you've been to college.

Poe's Law

This shouldn't be confused with the Internet adage coined by Nathan Poe (see page 180 in the Online section). The Poe in question here is Edgar Allan Poe (1809–49), author of such seminal pieces of Gothic horror as 'The Fall of the House of Usher' and 'The Pit and the Pendulum', as well as several mystery stories beginning with 'The Murders in the Rue Morgue', and featuring a detective, Auguste Dupin, who was a prototype for Sherlock Holmes. That these are all short stories is relevant to Poe's Law since it concerns the link between the length of a prose work or poem and its impact on the reader. For Poe believed that shorter was better. In an essay titled 'The Philosophy of Composition' (1846), he declared: 'If any literary work is too long to be read at one sitting, we must be content to dispense with the immensely important effect derivable from unity of impression – for, if two sittings be required, the affairs of the world interfere, and every thing like totality is at once destroyed.' By 'unity of effect' Poe was talking about the means necessary to produce an emotional impact, whether excitement, fear, wonder and so on. In the same essay Poe formulated the idea more precisely and this has sometimes been referred to as his law, one that he explicitly applied to poetry but which he thought applied to other literary forms as well:

It appears evident, then, that there is a distinct limit, as regards length, to all works of literary art – the limit of a single sitting.

Art and design

The Cow Rule

Animals can fetch high prices, especially when they are hung, drawn and quartered. In 1991 art collector and ex-husband of

Nigella Lawson, Charles Saatchi, paid Damien Hirst £50,000 for his most famous work, 'The Physical Impossibility of Death in the Mind of Someone Living', a 14-foot tiger shark preserved in formaldehyde and floating in a glass case. When Saatchi sold it[14] in 2004 to a Connecticut hedge-fund manager the price of the dead shark had jumped from under $100,000 to $8 million, although the title of a book by Don Thompson, *The $12 Million Stuffed Shark*, suggests that the sum might be half as high again. In a more traditional field of animal depiction, an oil painting of a horse called Gimcrack by the eighteenth-century artist George Stubbs was recently sold at Christie's in London for more than £22 million.

So animals sell, and they sell well. But there is a hierarchy of value[15] in such pictures which means that pure-bred dogs are worth more than mongrels, and racehorses carry a higher price tag than carthorses. According to the author Don Thompson, mentioned above, the value of a painting which includes game birds depends on how much it costs to hunt the real-life birds: a grouse goes for three times as much as a mallard. And there is a

---

[14] The original shark had started to decay and when Hirst learned that Saatchi was selling it the artist offered to do another and more carefully preserved version for the new buyer. As Hirst pointed out, that raised the question of whether a copy could have the same significance as the original. However, since he is a conceptual artist, the question presumably didn't detain him for very long.

[15] There is also a hierarchy in human portraits, especially when the artist is not famous and people are buying merely to have something interesting or decorative to hang on their walls. According to one auctioneer, the least likely ones to sell are depictions of grumpy old men, followed by serious-looking older ladies. Attractive younger women do well, though not necessarily as well as children, where girls tend to outsell boys.

final rule, according to the New York dealer David Nash, which states that:

> Paintings with cows never do well. Never.

Laver's Law

James Laver (1899–1975) was a writer and a historian of fashion who worked at the Victoria & Albert Museum. Emerging from a strict religious background – at Oxford he produced a thesis on John Wesley, founder of Methodism – Laver was also the author of *Nymph Errant* (1932), a best-seller regarded as slightly scandalous at the time and turned into a musical by Cole Porter. Laver applied quite serious methods to the study of fashion, even evolving a philosophy of the subject and speculating that the height of waistlines could be related to times of war (see also Hemline Theory in Economics). Laver's Law, which he formulated during the 1930s, is a handy guide to how styles in women's dress will be regarded over a period of more than a century and a half. According to Laver's Law, any item will be seen as:

- Indecent 10 years before its time
- Shameless 5 years before its time
- Daring 1 year before its time
- Smart during its time in fashion
- Dowdy 1 year after its time
- Hideous 10 years after its time
- Ridiculous 20 years after its time

- Amusing 30 years after its time
- Quaint 50 years after its time
- Charming 70 years after its time
- Romantic 100 years after its time
- Beautiful 150 years after its time

Do these still apply? Maybe not so neatly in the speeded-up and more chaotic world of contemporary fashion where six months ago might be classed as 'dowdy'. But try the 'amusing' test on the big-hair, big-shoulders fashions of the 1980s and the 'quaint' test on the flared, flower-powered 1960s. Nor does Laver's Law have to be restricted to fashion. With its underlying notions of cyclical taste and cultural patterns, it can also be applied to such fields as architecture and music.

4

Science

Science is the natural home of laws, theories, rules and principles. Most of them are best left to specialists but I have selected a few that have a general application or are connected to a particular scientist or have a quirky appeal. You will have to look elsewhere for the hard stuff like Einstein's theories and even the older and elementary principles propounded by Newton or Archimedes. This is the lighter, more personal end of science.

The laws of sci-fi writers

Asimov's Laws of Robotics

The science-fiction writer Isaac Asimov (1920–92) first formulated these laws of fictional robots in a short story published in the early 1940s. The laws are for 'good' robots and they sprang from Asimov's desire to have his readers see the potential in new technology rather than being afraid of out-of-control scientific development.

First Law: A robot may not injure a human being, or, through inaction, allow a human being to come to harm.

Second Law: A robot must obey orders given to it by human beings, except where such orders would conflict with the First Law.

Third Law: A robot must protect its own existence as long as such protection does not conflict with the First or Second Law.

As with real-life laws, Asimov's robot rules were subject to revision and commentary, and the writer added to and refined them in various stories. The laws also create dilemmas. What happens if a robot obeying the First Law has to injure one human being in order to protect another? How does it decide between the two humans? And does a robot have to follow any order from a human being, even if the order is given by a child – or an idiot?

In the years since Asimov laid down the laws, robots have become familiar players in sci-fi, whether as the heroic and villainous androids of the *Terminator* films or the more ambiguous presentations of *Blade Runner* and the *Alien* series. But the purpose of Asimov's laws wasn't just to reassure the technophobes. Robots were imaginary in the 1940s and Asimov's laws showed that the creation of an imagined world – whether it is a utopia, a dystopia or simply a middle-earth – needs structure and consistency.

But fiction, especially when it's of the science variety, has a habit of eventually turning into fact. In 2012 the European

Union launched the RoboLaw Project as a way of opening up discussion on proposals for the laws and regulations that will be necessary to manage the emerging robotics technologies.[1] Not only were robot-building engineers and lawyers consulted but also philosophers because of the moral and ethical aspects of using robots in, for example, the care of children or older people. Interesting questions emerge: ones of liability and autonomy. If a driverless car crashes, then who pays? Or, if what is called an 'assistive exoskeleton' is involved in someone's death, then who or what is at fault? If robots are granted autonomy, do they also have rights and responsibilities? For example, if a robot were enabled to perform legal transactions by being given the same sort of status which corporations have, then the problem arises of how it could legally be represented in court. More than seventy years after they were first proposed, Asimov's Laws aren't going to go away. Rather, they are going to get a lot more complex.

Arthur C. Clarke's Laws

The British science-fiction writer Arthur C. Clarke (1917–2008) was an optimistic, visionary writer in a tradition of sci-fi realism that now seems, sadly, to have gone out of fashion. He conceived awe-inspiring scenarios, as in his collaboration with Stanley Kubrick on the story and film *2001* (1968) or in *Rendezvous with Rama* (1973), his novel of humanity's first encounter with alien

---

[1] Its report 'Guidelines on Regulating Robotics' was issued on 22 September 2014 and can be downloaded.

intelligence in the shape of a 50-kilometre cylindrical starship that floats into the solar system and then floats out again.

Clarke kept well away from fantasy, and his work is solidly grounded in physics and probability even in his most outlandish suggestions, as in the giant 'space elevator' he dreamed up in *The Fountains of Paradise* (1979), a snaky tube connecting earth to a geo-stationary satellite many thousands of miles overhead. Indeed, Clarke enjoyed teasing people with the idea that, if science did have limits, then they were far beyond anything which we could envisage. He produced plenty of non-fiction and in a collection of essays published for the 2000 millennium he reiterated that '"Impossible" is an extremely dangerous word', so dangerous that it had earlier led him to propound three laws. They are as follows:

1   When a distinguished but elderly[2] scientist states that something is possible, (s)he is almost certainly right. When (s)he states that something is impossible, (s)he is very probably wrong.[3]

2   The only way of discovering the limits of the possible is to venture a little way past them into the impossible.

---

[2] Arthur C. Clarke had a narrow and sardonic definition of 'elderly': 'In physics and mathematics it means over thirty [. . .] as every researcher just out of college knows, scientists of over fifty are good for nothing but board meetings and should at all costs be kept out of the laboratory . . .'

[3] Sci-fi writer Isaac Asimov (see also Asimov's laws of robotics) produced a corollary to Clarke's first law which goes as follows: 'When, however, the lay public rallies round an idea that is denounced by distinguished but elderly scientists and supports that idea with great fervor and emotion – the distinguished but elderly scientists are then, after all, probably right.'

3 Any sufficiently advanced technology is indistinguishable from magic.

As an example of the third and most frequently quoted law, Clarke said that while he would have believed anyone who told him back in 1962 that there would one day exist a book-sized object capable of holding the contents of an entire library, he would never have accepted that the same device could find a page or word in a second and then convert it into any typeface and size from Albertus Extra Bold to Zurich Calligraphic. After all, as Clarke wrote in explanation, he was old enough to remember seeing and hearing the Linotype machines which slowly converted 'molten lead into front pages that required two men to lift them'.

As often, a law which is neatly formulated encourages other people to come up with variations that are intended to be witty or thought-provoking or both. Clarke's third law prompted Michael Shermer to compose one about alien intelligence or extra-terrestrial intelligence (ETI) in a column in *Scientific American.*

Any sufficiently advanced ETI is indistinguishable from God.

Shermer's point is that, given the rapidity of technological advance (see Moore's Law in Online), any alien intelligence capable of making contact with humanity would be so far ahead of us that he/she/it would seem god-like. On a more mundane level, there is also Grey's Law, even if the identity of Grey is obscure. Obviously under the influence of Clarke's formulation, Grey's Law states that:

> Any sufficiently advanced incompetence is indistinguishable from malice.

The Odd Man Theory

Michael Crichton (1942–2008) was one of the most successful writers of the last half-century. Creator of the Jurassic Park franchise, Crichton was a medical doctor who from the beginning of his writing career was tirelessly productive, turning out five novels in 1968–69 alone. His first big hit was the second of the 1969 novels, *The Andromeda Strain*, in which a deadly extraterrestrial microbe is carried to earth on a returning satellite. At an underground facility in the Nevada desert, equipped with its own atomic device, scientists battle to counter the mutating Andromeda microbe. If the contamination threatens to escape, an automatic destruction sequence is initiated. By intention, only one scientist is equipped with the key to halt the process. The choice of key-holder is the result of what's referred to as the Robertson Odd Man Hypothesis. All of this is made up but, in keeping with Crichton's scientific background and careful research, it sounds plausible. In the words of one of the characters in the 1971 film version of the novel, the Odd Man Hypothesis tells us that:

> An unmarried, male should carry out command decisions involving thermonuclear destruct contexts.

The Odd Man Theory has been broadened to suggest that:

Unmarried men are better able to execute the best, most dispassionate decisions in crises.

Of course in both book and film the microbe does escape and the unmarried scientist does manoeuvre his way through a battery of lasers to shut down the atomic device (because the scientists have belatedly worked out that a detonation will only cause the microbe to mutate faster and more furiously). Fortunately, Andromeda's final mutation is benign and it escapes back into the upper atmosphere. In the real world, a 'two-man rule' obtains in some critical sites such as missile silos or nuclear-armed submarines, by which two authorized personnel are needed to initiate the process of launching a missile.

Niven's Law

Few areas of science fiction (and possibly science fact) are as mind-bendingly complicated as time travel. The subject, and its tortuous possibilities, have been at the heart of sci-fi ever since H. G. Wells introduced both the expression and the concept of *The Time Machine* in his pioneering novel of 1895. Then at the beginning of the twentieth century Albert Einstein shook the world, or at least that tiny bit of it which could understand him, with concepts including the space–time continuum and the idea that an object in motion experiences time at a slower rate than an object at rest. (An astronaut who's been on a one-year trip into space will come back 0.022 seconds less old than her husband who has stayed behind on earth.) The concept of time, which had always seemed so absolute and regular, has started to become flexible.

It's more than a hundred years since Einstein proposed his theory of special relativity, and in that (space)time, the notion of time-travel has been treated at every level from the scholarly to the frivolous. But many key questions remain unanswered, and the most important of these must be: is it actually possible to travel in time? According to a law propounded by sci-fi writer Larry Niven[4] (b. 1938), it is not. In a 1973 essay titled 'The Theory and Practice of Time Travel', Niven stated that:

> If the universe of discourse permits the possibility of time travel and of changing the past, then no time machine will be invented in that universe.

Niven's essay is wackier than this rather formal declaration suggests but, in essence, his argument seems to boil down to this. If it is possible to create a time-machine and then travel back into history, then the (probably multiple) trips made into the past would create various potential futures since people would, either deliberately or accidentally,[5] do something that inevitably alters

---

[4] Larry Niven is famous for his 'laws', which range from the wryly humorous ('Never throw shit at an armed man' or 'Never fire a laser at a mirror') to the paradoxical ('The ways of being human are bounded but infinite').

[5] In the imagining of time travel, the smallest things can have giant, unforeseen consequences. In Ray Bradbury's short story 'A Sound of Thunder', a party returns to prehistory to go safari hunting a tyrannosaurus rex. Only those animals which are due to die – for example, after being struck by a falling tree – can be killed by the hunters, with all the bullets being removed afterwards so that no trace of human intervention remains to alter the course of history. One of the hunters steps off a

the course of history. Or, as Niven puts it: 'Every trip into the past means that all the dice have to be thrown over again.' Each change, however small, entails other changes until by a process of chance we arrive a state of affairs – a different universe – in which the time machine has not been invented. Hence there will be no means of travelling backwards in time.

Benford's Law

This one is connected to Sayre's Law (see page 191) in that it comments wryly on the connections between knowledge, strength of feeling and controversy. It was coined by the science-fiction writer and astrophysicist, Gregory Benford (b. 1941). In his fine novel, *Timescape* (1980), which makes ingenious use of the Kennedy assassination, he has a character reflect that:

> Passion is inversely proportional to the amount of real information available.

Benford's Law suggests that there will rarely be fiery disputes among scientists working in the same field because they are dealing with facts which are known and agreed upon. But in areas such as politics, where facts are thin on the ground and often disputed, feelings run high. This should not be confused

---

floating walkway and accidentally crushes a butterfly. When the safari party returns to the present, they find many changes from a different form of English and a different candidate winning a recent presidential election. Bradbury's story shows the perils of time-travel and is a literal example of the 'butterfly effect', even though the phrase itself hadn't been coined at the time.

with the other Benford's Law sometimes known as the First-Digit Law (see below).

Sturgeon's Law

Genre writers, whether of mysteries and thrillers or of sci-fi or romance, are used to being attacked or overlooked because the work they produce is automatically assumed to be inferior to 'serious' fiction. Sometimes they adopt a defensive, even apologetic tone, conscious that whatever they are doing will never be received with respect and even reverence accorded to serious fiction and other proper works of art. But occasionally a genre writer will go onto the attack, as Theodore Sturgeon did when he coined the law which usually appears, even in the *Oxford English Dictionary*, in the following no-nonsense form.

90% of everything is crap.

This may not be quite so damning or disillusioned as it sounds. In a feature for the September 1957 issue of the magazine *Venture Science Fiction* and talking of himself in the third person, Sturgeon (1918–85) recalled how he'd had a revelation: 'It came to him that sf [science fiction] is indeed ninety-percent crud, but that also – Eureka! – ninety-percent of everything is crud. All things – cars, books, cheeses, hairstyles, people and pins are, to the expert and discerning eye, crud, except for the acceptable tithe which we each happen to like.'

Sturgeon had made the same 90 per cent point at sci-fi conventions but, enshrined in print, his Law has extended its reach to apply not merely to genre fiction but to other areas such as Internet information. Sturgeon, also labelled as a law, a more gnomic observation which first appeared in a sci-fi magazine and which states that 'Nothing is absolutely so.'

Heinlein's rules

The science-fiction writer Robert Heinlein (1907–88) produced a set of no-nonsense rules in an essay 'On the Writing of Speculative Fiction' (1947). These are nothing to do with style or content but are a brisk reminder that if you want to be more than a would-be writer, you must actually sit down and write something rather than just thinking/dreaming/talking about doing it. Then, once it's finished, you must sell it and keep selling it.

Rule One: You Must Write

Rule Two: Finish What Your Start

Rule Three: You Must Refrain From Rewriting, Except to Editorial Order

Rule Four: You Must Put Your Story on the Market

Rule Five: You Must Keep it on the Market until it has Sold

Rule Three stands out as a non-commercial one and goes against the almost universal view that at least some degree of revision and rewriting is a good thing. Most likely, Robert Heinlein was being provocative. But the rule may also spring from his pulp-fiction magazine days, where stories had to be produced quickly and rewriting was a luxury he simply couldn't afford. Like other sci-fi writers such as Larry Niven and Jerry Pournelle (see Pournelle's Law on page 192), Heinlein had a dogmatic style of laying down his 'laws', one which contrasts with the often less assertive style of writers in other genres.

Some eponymous laws

Stigler's Law of Eponomy

There is no better place to begin exploring eponymously named scientific laws than one which questions the very principles behind the naming process. How can one gain immortality or, at least, long-lasting fame? Perhaps by building a tower (Donald Trump springs to mind) or creating a vacuum cleaner (the Dyson) or – negatively – by committing a series of terrible crimes. But if anyone is guaranteed an eternal name it must surely be the scientist who makes a fundamental discovery or establishes a new truth and whose name is forever after enshrined in X's Law or Y's Theory. The trouble is that, according to Stigler's Law of Eponomy, things rarely happen so neatly.

In 1980 Stephen Stigler, a statistics professor at the University of Chicago, was invited to contribute to a *festschrift* for the sociologist Robert K. Merton, who among much else developed the Law of Unintended Consequences (see page 43). Merton had also written about the way in which discoveries in science often occur simultaneously in different places or have several originators. With this in mind, Stigler came up with a law which, in essence, states that:

No scientific discovery is named after its original discoverer.

According to Stigler, laws are rarely attributed to living people but are usually named by a scientific community which is unlikely to investigate too closely who first originated an idea. Also, scientists commemorated with eponymous laws are often being honoured for their general achievements and status rather than a particular moment of discovery to which others have probably contributed. By intention, Stigler's Law is an example of itself, since it could as well be termed Merton's Law.

And that is not the end of it, since there is an earlier observation termed Boyer's Law (by H. C. Kennedy) that 'Mathematical formulas and theorems are usually not named after their original discoverers.'

Examples of Stigler's Law in this book include Gresham's Law and the Bechdel Rule. What all this regressive and self-reflective stuff goes to show is that 'there is nothing new under the sun' (anonymous). Or, in a more elegant variation, 'True Wit is Nature to advantage dress'd/What oft was thought, but ne'er so well express'd' (Alexander Pope).

Benford's Law

Imagine that you are a forensic accountant – yes, such experts do exist – examining a batch of figures and trying to determine whether they are genuine or fraudulent by the simple process of glancing down at the first digit in each set of numbers. What would you expect to find? That, if you had a sufficiently large sample, then every number between 1 and 9 would occur as a first digit in roughly equivalent amounts, slightly more than 10 per cent in each case? Common sense suggests just such an even distribution. And what apparent anomaly would rouse your suspicions? To discover that one or two digits – say, the numbers 1 and 2 – predominated at the expense of the others in your list? Curiously, exactly the opposite is true. A seemingly random collection of numbers beginning in equal quantities from 1 through to 9 may actually be evidence of fraud, while a concentration of 1s, 2s and 3s at the beginning of a set of number sequences is strongly suggestive that what you're looking at is genuine.

This insight, which is sometimes known as the First-Digit Law, is credited to Frank Benford (1883–1948), a physicist working at the General Electric Research Laboratory in Schenectady, New York. In 1938, Benford noticed something curious about the logarithm books in the lab. (Log books or tables were used for calculations in pre-electronic days.) Benford realized that the early sections of the log books, those which contained number sequences starting with the digits 1 or 2, were more scuffed and worn than the later sections listing numbers beginning with 7s or 8s or 9s. In fact, the same thought, also prompted by log books, had occurred more than fifty years earlier to the US astronomer, Simon Newcomb, but Benford took the insight much further. Wondering whether he had stumbled upon some odd if baffling truth, he began to look at various sets of data, anything from river catchment areas to baseball statistics to the numbers mentioned on the front page of *The New York Times* and town populations, as well as such out-of-the-way figures as those featuring in the street addresses of the first 342 people listed in the book 'American Men of Science' or electricity bills in the Solomon Islands.

In all such cases, Benford discovered, the number 1 appeared as the initial digit about 30 per cent of the time. This led to the formulation of Benford's Law:

> The probability that a number randomly selected from a table of physical constants or statistical data will start with a '1' is about 0.3 (rather than the 0.1 probability to be expected if all digits were equally likely).

But it doesn't stop there. If there is nearly a one-in-three chance that any random number drawn from a wide enough sample of numbers will start with a 1, then around 18 per cent will start with a '2', just over 12 per cent with a '3' and so on down. Less than 5 per cent of such numbers will begin with a '9'. These findings apply to naturally generated data, such as website statistics or stock prices or bank balances. If such figures don't obey Benford's Law then there is probably something wrong with them. Of course, the Law does not apply to all sets of figures, for example a restricted list such as the ages of US presidents when they are elected, or to assigned digits such as street numbers or telephone numbers. But it has enough predictive validity to be used as a tool in uncovering fraud and misreporting.

There are explanations for Benford's Law but they are dense and mathematical, and it may be that the average law-hunter is happy just to bask in the mystery and peculiarity of this one. As a footnote and prompted by the fact that, among all the data he examined, Benford looked at the figures on the front page of *The New York Times*, I decided to test out his Law on the day when I happened to be writing this piece (31 October 2014). I took the front page of *The Guardian*. There were three headline stories, each of them continuing on an inside page. One story was to do with MI6 and contained no numbers at all apart from the '6' and a reference to the year 2004. Another reported an attack by a literary agent on Amazon's digital monopoly, and included only a single figure (30 per cent). The third and biggest piece, illustrated with a picture of a masked health worker in Freetown, Sierra Leone, was about the Ebola outbreak that began in West Africa. It included several sets of figures: at that point in the end of October, there had been 5,235 probable and suspected cases of the disease in Sierra Leone, out of 13,703 worldwide and 1,500 deaths. The Freetown call centre dealing with calls was receiving 1,300 a day. The specialist in charge had 135 staff; there were 117 hotlines; a treatment centre had 100 beds. The only figure apart from the total of cases (5,235) to buck the one-comes-first pattern was a reference to someone's age (24).

So it seems as though Benford's Law really does rule.

(See above for Benford's Law (of Controversy) – no relation.)

Langmuir's Laws of Bad Science

If a scientific theory is to be considered valid, then it has to fulfil two principal and related criteria: the theory must be testable and it must be capable of being falsified. Anyone can advance the theory that God exists but the theory can never achieve the status of a scientific proposition because there is no way of proving (or disproving) the belief. A scientific theory, on the other hand, must be held up to the light. If it is tested often enough, and still holds true (i.e. by giving the same results under the same conditions), then that theory will be on its way to becoming a law. In this way Isaac Newton's theories about gravity both fitted general observation – objects fall down rather than float up – as well as being testable by experiment, and thus acquired the status of laws, even if they were modified by later theories such as Einstein's.

But there are also areas where science intersects with belief systems which may be religious or cultural, as in the debate about evolution and intelligent design or the arguments over global warming, and these contested spaces gives scope for plenty of what's known as bad science.

Irving Langmuir (1881–1957) was an American chemist and physicist who won the Nobel prize for Chemistry in 1932 and spent his working life at the General Electric Company in Schenectady, New York, like Frank Benford (see Benford's Law above). He was also a campaigner against 'pathological science', a term he used to describe the way in which preconception, bias or wishful thinking could affect scientific research. In 1953 during what was described as a 'colloquium' at General Electric's Knolls Atomic Power Laboratory he detailed the kinds of pitfall into which scientists could stumble if they didn't take care over their methods. Among other topics, he touched on research into extrasensory perception and flying saucers, a major preoccupation of the 1950s. Langmuir concluded that most the unidentified flying object (UFO) sightings 'were Venus seen in the evening through a murky atmosphere'. Out of this session emerged Langmuir's Symptoms of Pathological Science, later known as his eponymous laws. They are arranged chronologically to show how after a deluded idea takes hold, it is then defended more and more wildly until it fades away to nothing:

1   The maximum effect that is observed [in an experiment] is produced by a causative agent of barely detectable intensity, and the magnitude of the effect is substantially independent of the intensity of the cause.

2   The effect is of a magnitude that remains close to the limit of detectability, or many measurements are necessary because of the low level of significance of the results.

3   There are claims of great accuracy.

4   Fantastic theories contrary to experience are suggested.

5   Criticisms are met by ad hoc excuses thought up on the spur of the moment.

6   The ratio of supporters to critics rises to somewhere near 50 per cent and then falls gradually to zero.

As an example of the first two laws, Irving Langmuir described the research of Alexander Gurwitsch, a professor at a Moscow university in the 1920s, who believed that growing plants give off 'mitogenetic rays', a form of ultraviolet radiation supposedly capable of affecting development in neighbouring plants. This theory was 'tested' on onion roots. When one root was put to grow close to another, it appeared to change direction as if 'something' had travelled between the two. Yet, according to Langmuir, it made no difference if an extra source of ultraviolet light was added or if the number of onion roots was increased, though variations should have occurred as a result of these additions and been measurable under proper scientific procedure. Instead, 'it had to be just the amount of [ultraviolet] intensity that's given off by an onion root', no more and no less, thus demonstrating his first law that 'the magnitude of the effect is substantially independent of the intensity of the cause'. The magical mitogenetic belief then spread to encompass many 'living things' beyond onion roots.

In demonstration of his second law that the evidence is hard to detect and difficult to interpret, Langmuir tells of how 'then they started to use photoelectric cells to check it, and whatever they did they practically always found that if you got the conditions just right, you could just detect [mitogenetic rays] and prove it. But if you looked over those photographic plates that showed this ultraviolet light you found that the amount of light was not much bigger than the natural particles of the photographic plate so that people could have different opinions as to whether it did or did not show this effect.'

Langmuir's other laws are to do with natural human exaggeration about the validity and significance of the theories followed by defensiveness on the part of the scientists when they are attacked, until finally support for the theories has completely drained away. Langmuir emphasized that there was no dishonesty involved; it is more a case of people, including scientists who are trained to be objective, seeing what they wanted to see.

Littlewood's Law

Have you ever encountered an unusual word or piece of information, and then very soon afterwards come across it for a second time, and a bit later even a third? The term 'frequency illusion' is the technical expression for the phenomenon whereby such a repetition will stick in the memory as if it is part of a pattern or 'more than coincidence' even though the prosaic explanation is that, having once been alerted to something out-of-the-way, we are unconsciously keeping an eye or an ear open for it to crop up again. And if/when it does, that is merely confirmation that this new mysterious thing is, somehow, omnipresent. A less official (and somewhat odder) term for the frequency illusion is the 'Baader-Meinhof phenomenon', apparently coined in 1994 during an online discussion and so called by a contributor who'd come across the name of the extreme-left German terrorist group twice within 24 hours. And if you haven't heard of the Baader-Meinhof gang before, don't worry, because in accordance with the Baader-Meinhof phenomenon you'll surely be hearing about them again very soon.

There are various related scientific theories which seek to explain coincidences and cases of synchronicity (as when you are thinking of someone only to be rung moments later by the very person who was just on your mind), explanations which do away with any psychic shading or supernatural tinge. Perhaps the most arresting of these theories is Littlewood's Law, named after John Littlewood (1885–1977), a Cambridge mathematician whose posthumously published collection of essays introduced the notion that:

> A typical person will experience about one miracle a month during his or her lifetime.

The proof of the law goes like this: on the assumption that we are truly awake and alert to our environment for about eight hours a day, we will see and hear different or discrete things happening around us at about the rate of one per second. The total number of such 'events' works out at around 30,000 a day or approaching a million a month. The *Oxford English Dictionary* gives one definition of miracle as a 'remarkable' or 'very surprising' event; in other words, a one-in-a-million occurrence. On this basis, by witnessing nearly a million 'events' every thirty days or so, we are statistically likely to experience a monthly miracle.

Of course, belief in Littlewood's Law depends on accepting the idea that our daily experience can be chopped up into very small and discrete sections, or events, and also on a non-religious interpretation of 'miracle' as something very rare and remarkable though not caused by supernatural agency. But John Littlewood was really making the rational point that unusual things, even outrageous coincidences, do happen, and that these fall within statistical parameters. To go back to the I-was-just-thinking-about-you-and-now-you've-rung example, the real explanation isn't the spooky, psychic one but rather to consider the many occasions on which the act of thinking of someone will not be followed by the phone ringing. Or, if the phone does go, it will turn out to be a call from a different person altogether. These calls we don't note afterwards because they are not coincidences or examples of synchronicity.

Saffo's Thirty-Year Rule

Paul Saffo (b. 1954) is a Silicon Valley forecaster, peering into the future, foreseeing changes and advising on their impact. As long ago as 1992 he was looking at the time it takes for a new piece of technology to become familiar and, in a feature in *Design World* magazine, he formulated the following rule:

> It takes about 30 years for a new idea to fully seep into our culture.

Saffo also observed that what he termed 'macro-myopia' operates with any new technology. At first its potential is overestimated and so expectations are inflated; then when those initial expectations aren't met, disappointment and frustration set in with the result that the long-term impact of the innovation is underestimated.[6] As an example, he refers

---

[6] Researcher and scientist Roy Amara made a similar observation – 'We tend to overestimate the effect of a technology in the short run and underestimate the effect in the long run' – which is sometimes referred to as Amara's Law.

to predictions made in the late 1970s that every home would soon have its own computer. When that hadn't happened by the mid-1980s, many computer companies abandoned the home market, until Nintendo showed the way by providing home entertainment devices. The success of a new technology also depends on cultural understanding and acceptance, something which may involve overturning early assumptions made by the innovators and pioneer users. In the beginning, radio was regarded as both a transmitter and a receiver and it did not really take off as a new medium until it was treated as something to listen to, rather than communicate from. In the early days, the future of flight was seen as a matter of personal, not mass, transport, and even as late as the 1950s cartoon-style visions of the future show dozens of mini-planes and heli-machines flitting about the sky, carrying the individual commuter to work.

Paul Saffo broke down the various stages in his thirty-year rule like this: 'First decade: lots of excitement, lots of puzzlement, not a lot of penetration. Second decade: lots of flux, penetration of the product into society is beginning. Third decade: "Oh, so what?" Just a standard technology and everybody has it.'

(See also 'Thirty-year Rule' in Politics)

Orgel's Rule

British-born chemist and biologist Leslie Orgel (1927–2007) is remembered for two rules, the first of which is (for the non-scientist) a fairly specialized observation about protein. But

Orgel's Second Rule is snappier and more comprehensible. It says simply:

Evolution is cleverer than you.

Human beings are intelligent but no match for the millions of years of intricate development which lies behind evolution. So, if some aspect of natural development seems baffling or pointless to a professional scientist, then the fault is much more likely to be not with nature but with the expert who has not yet grasped the function of some particularly ingenious piece of design. This is Orgel's Second Rule applied to an evolutionary detail. It can also stand as an implicit rebuke to the idea of 'intelligent design', the euphemistic term for creationism or belief in some overseeing, divine intelligence which is responsible for life on earth. There is no need for a creator since evolution is doing the work.

General science

Planetary naming rules

Did you imagine that if a new heavenly body happened to swim into your telescopic vision as you were star-gazing one night, then you could name it after yourself or your first family pet? Well, if it's within the solar system, you'll have to think again. The naming of the planets and everything connected to them is governed by a strict set of rules, overseen by the International Astronomical Union (IAU) and applying not only to self-contained bodies such as satellites but the much larger category of topographical features such as craters, fissures, mountains, scarps and plains. In shortened form the most important of these IAU rules are:

1   Nomenclature is a tool and the first consideration should be to make it simple, clear and unambiguous.

2   In general, official names will not be given to features whose longest dimensions are less than 100 metres, although exceptions may be made for smaller features having exceptional scientific interest.

3   The number of names chosen for each body should be kept to a minimum. Features should be named only when they have special scientific interest.

4   Duplication of the same surface feature name on two or more bodies, and of the same name for satellites and minor planets, is discouraged.

5   Individual names chosen for each body should be expressed in the language of origin.

6   Where possible, the themes established in early solar system nomenclature should be used and expanded on.

7   Solar system nomenclature should be international in its choice of names. [. . .] Where appropriate, the WGPSN (Working Group for Planetary System Nomenclature) strongly supports an equitable selection of names from ethnic groups, countries, and gender on each map;

however, a higher percentage of names from the country planning a landing is allowed on landing site maps.

8   No names having political, military or religious significance may be used, except for names of political figures prior to the nineteenth century.

9   Commemoration of persons on planetary bodies should not normally be a goal in itself, but may be employed in special circumstances and is reserved for persons of high and enduring international standing. Persons being so honored must have been deceased for at least three years.

Within these official rules are to be found some quirks and curiosities. For example:

Size in rule 2: Craters on Mars which are less than 60km in diameter are named after towns on earth with populations of less than 100,000. So Mars is home to Albany, Banff, Edam (the Dutch town, not the cheese), Maidstone, Pompeii, and Tooting Craters, the last of which was discovered in 2005 and named for the London suburb where its discoverer was born. The 100,000 population limit is not observed too strictly: Bristol and Johannesburg craters are named after cities with populations several times that number.

Names from ethnic groups in rule 7: The Kuiper Belt – a vast ring of 'ice' objects floating at the outskirts of the solar system – is named after its discoverer, the astronomer Gerard Kuiper (1905–73). Pluto, which recently suffered the indignity of being downgraded from the status of full planet to dwarf planet, is one of these Kuiper Belt Objects (KBOs) as they are known. The custom is to name KBOs after goddesses from various cultures, some of them fertility figures, perhaps because the Belt is thought to be made up of debris left over from the formation of the solar system. So, billions of miles beyond the earth, there float Makemake and Haumea (both from Polynesian creation myths), Sedna, the Inuit goddess of the sea, and Eris, the Greek goddess of strife, who was thought an appropriate choice since her discovery was made around the time of debate over the status of Pluto and other KBOs.

Dead names in rule 9: Some deceased Russian cosmonauts are commemorated by craters in and around Mare Moscoviense while their American counterparts, such as those killed in the 1981 Space Shuttle disaster, are remembered in the names given to craters in or near the larger Apollo crater. To date, no nationals other than Russians and Americans have landed on the moon but, if and when they do, the IAU guide to planetary nomenclature gives this assurance: 'Appropriate locations will be provided in the future for other space-faring nations should they also suffer casualties.' It's rather like leaving a blank space on a gravestone.

Six rules of street naming . . .

It's a bit of a jump, perhaps, from the rules which govern the names of planetary features to those which determine street names and house numbering. Yet, though there may not be much science involved, there is certainly a degree of logic and a dash of arithmetic, and street nomenclature is somewhat closer to home than the outer planets.

The name of the street where you live may affect your ability to sell your property, according to a survey conducted in 2014 which found that while living somewhere with a suggestive name such as Crotch Crescent or Slag Lane might raise a snigger, it can also lower the selling price by almost a quarter in comparison with a more conventionally named street in the same neighbourhood. Yet you may be stuck with it since there are often historical reasons for a name and, unless all the residents agree, it can be difficult to change it.

New streets in new developments are a different matter, though, and here there are distinct rules. It's a more complicated subject than the casual onlooker might think, and what follows applies only to England. Every council and local authority has guidelines on how streets should be named and these differ slightly in their detail and in the examples of those names which are appropriate and those which are to be avoided. These rules are a summary of the general state of things:

1   No street or building name can start with 'The'.

2   New streets must not duplicate an existing street name or be very similar in name or sound (e.g. Manor Lane/ Manor Road; Churchill Road/Birch Hill Street) so as to avoid confusion for the emergency services, deliveries and so on.

3   Streets may occasionally be named after people who are deceased, but the preference is for the dead person

to have some connection to the area. (Exceptions may be made for saints or members of the royal family.) Permission to use the name is always needed from any living relatives. Streets should not be named after people who are still alive.[7]

4   Street names should not be difficult to pronounce or awkward to spell. In general, words of more than three syllables are to be avoided and two words should not be used except in special cases. Numeric characters should not be used in street names and the apostrophe is discouraged.

5   Names which have a commercial connection or which are otherwise unsuitable, frivolous, obscene or liable to misinterpretation ought to be avoided.[8]

6   The use of North, South, East or West (as in Alfred Road North and Alfred Road South or East or West) is only acceptable where the road is continuous and passes a major junction. It is not acceptable when the road is in two separate parts with no vehicular access between the two. In such a case one half should be completely renamed.

---

[7] Northumberland Borough Council is very clear about why this is not a good idea: 'A living person's name cannot be used in case that person commits an offence resulting in a prison sentence.'

[8] Durham Council states that 'Street names that may be open to re-interpretation by graffiti or shortening of the name shall be avoided' while the Royal Borough of Kingston upon Thames offers the following helpful examples of what not to choose: 'unsuitable names such as Garrison Lane, Ordnance Way, Tip House, or names capable of deliberate misinterpretation such as Austyn Close or Hoare Way.'

. . . and three rules on numbering houses

This is also quite complicated because of the problems of numbering when it comes to multi-occupied properties or large blocks of flats. However, there are a few simple rules which apply in England, as below:

1   A new street should be numbered with even numbers on one side and odd numbers on the other, except for a cul-de-sac where consecutive numbering in a clockwise direction is preferred.

2   The correct numerical sequence will be used for street numbering and no exceptions will be made for any numbers.[9]

3   Buildings (including those on corner sites) are numbered according to the street that the main entrance appears on. Any manipulation of numbering to obtain a different address is not acceptable.[10]

Law of Urination

A group of scientists from the Georgia Institute of Technology in Atlanta started employing high-speed video to find out how

---

[9] You cannot choose to be numbered with a lucky 7 or to avoid an unlucky 13 (though some authorities do allow for 13 to be 'excluded').

[10] You live in a house which has doors onto both Grove Avenue and Skid Row but if your main entrance opens onto the second of these then Skid Row is your address. And you cannot 'manipulate' numbers so as to get a prestige address, along the lines of Apsley House near Hyde Park, the residence of the first Duke of Wellington and also known as Number One, London.

animals and fluids interact. Among other investigations, they've looked into the way in which dogs shake themselves dry. And it was while videoing animals at their local zoo that they made another and curious discovery: almost regardless of the size of an animal, the time it took to pee was the same. Their research resulted in a paper published in 2013 and titled the 'Law of Urination'. Helpfully, the law was outlined as the second part of the title:

All mammals empty their bladders over the same duration.

Given that the bladder of a large dog can hold nearly one and half litres of fluid while an elephant's bladder can contain more than a hundred times that amount (that's to compare the holding capacity of a large bottle of soda against that of three dustbins), it seems surprising that both animals should spend an equivalent time relieving themselves. The same observation applies to intermediate animals such as goats or cows or the big cats.

The mystery of how a single time-frame could fit all sizes was solved by looking at the urinary tract measurements of the various animals. Along with larger bladders, larger animals also have urethras that are both longer and wider. An expanding length increases the force of gravity on the urine so that it goes faster, while a wider urethra means more urine leaves the body at the same time. These increases are correlated with body mass, with the result that an elephant can empty its bladder in about the same amount of time as a cat.

The rule does not apply to small mammals below a kilogram (or a little over two pounds) in weight. The urethras of creatures such as rats and mice are so short and narrow that surface tension in the urine slows down the flow to drops but even so, with very small bladders, they require a much shorter time to pee successfully. Such brief stops are also a defence against predators.

And the answers to the two questions which will be in your mind if you've got this far? Yes, the same time-frame applies to humans as to other mammals. And the average duration, as determined by the scientists at Atlanta's Georgia Tech is 21 seconds.

The Five-Second Rule

The urban legend/old-wives'-tale that it is safe to eat a piece of food which has dropped to the floor as long as it is picked up within five seconds seems to have some basis in reality. In 2014 researchers from Aston University in Birmingham reported on experiments in which they had brought together the three necessary ingredients for a trial: portions of food and different types of flooring together with varieties of bacteria. They then dropped toast, pasta, biscuits and sticky sweets onto carpeted, tiled and laminated surfaces which were infested with bacteria including e.coli, and left the food for between three and thirty seconds. Afterwards, Anthony Hilton, Professor of Microbiology at Aston reported that, although there was always a risk of infection, it was not that great: 'We have found evidence that transfer from indoor flooring surfaces is incredibly poor with carpet actually posing the lowest risk of bacterial transfer onto dropped food.' The two relevant findings relating to the Five-Second Rule are:

1   Time is a significant factor in the transfer of bacteria from a floor surface to a piece of food.

2   The type of flooring the food has been dropped on has an effect, with bacteria least likely to transfer from carpeted surfaces and most likely to transfer from laminate or tiled surfaces to moist foods making contact for more than five seconds.

Earlier American research at universities in Illinois and South Carolina seems to suggest that it's still a dangerous practice since dropped food picks up bacteria, however short the period, and that carpeting is a favoured spot for a bacterium such as salmonella. So whether you observe the Five-Second Rule or not may be down to which researchers you trust more. What all the experimenters were agreed on, however, was that women are marginally more likely to pick up fallen food than men, and that dropped chocolate will be more readily retrieved than a floppy stalk of broccoli.

The Red Queen Principle

In the research-and-development wings of every really large arms multinational there must be departments which are, in effect, working against each other. One batch of scientists is busy trying to improve the effectiveness of armour-piercing shot and shell while in another laboratory, maybe the very one next door, a second group will be coming up with ways to reinforce the same protective cladding that the first group wants to penetrate. On a small scale, this mimics the competition between defence departments in different countries as they constantly try to find ways of giving their forces that competitive edge which, once achieved, must be countered by complementary defensive/offensive measures from the other side. The end result, as it was during the Cold War, is an uneasy equilibrium.

The arms race business is an example of the Red Queen Principle. The name derives from the moment in Lewis Carroll's *Through the Looking Glass* (1871) when Alice, finding that she isn't getting anywhere despite running fast, complains: 'Well, in our country, [. . .] you'd generally get to somewhere else – if you ran very fast for a long time, as we've been doing.' To which the Queen's replies: 'A slow sort of country! [. . .] Now, here, you see, it takes all the running you can do, to keep in the same place. If you want to get somewhere else, you must run at least twice as fast as that!'

The Red Queen Principle or Hypothesis was proposed in 1973 by the US evolutionary biologist Leigh Van Valen (1935–2010). The underlying idea is that a species' fitness for survival is improved when it gains a competitive advantage over those other species to which its own continued existence is linked. The most obvious example is the connection between predator and prey. Rabbits that run faster are better protected against predatory foxes – until the foxes improve their offensive technique and start running faster too. As with the global arms race or Alice's case in *Through the Looking Glass*, a rough equilibrium or stasis is thus maintained even if this illusory calm can be achieved only by some frantic pedalling under the surface. So one could sum up the Red Queen Principle as: although it may look as though you're standing still, standing still is not an option. More formally it could be expressed as:

Organisms must constantly adapt and evolve to guarantee their survival against opposing organisms which are themselves continuously adapting and changing.

The Laws of Thermodynamics

In general this book avoids 'proper' scientific laws partly because they are often very specialist as well as being hard to explain. But an exception is being made for the Laws of Thermodynamics because, unlikely as it may seem, they once made the headlines, at least in more highbrow publications. The story is below.

The novelist and academic C. P. Snow (1905–80) is pretty well forgotten now but he was a big figure in his day. A Cambridge academic, civil servant and adviser to governments, he wrote an eleven-novel sequence called *Stranger and Brothers*, which is partly autobiographical. The title of one of the volumes is *Corridors of Power*, a phrase which Snow was responsible for popularizing. In a 1959 lecture titled 'The Two Cultures' – another expression which Snow popularized – Snow focused on the disastrous gap between the arts and the sciences. He particularly disliked what he saw as the condescending attitude of some non-scientists:

A good many times I have been present at gatherings of people who, by the standards of the traditional culture, are thought highly educated and who have with considerable gusto been expressing their incredulity at the illiteracy of scientists. Once or twice I have been provoked and have asked the company how many of them could describe the Second Law of Thermodynamics. The response was cold: it was also negative. Yet I was asking something which is the scientific equivalent of: Have you read a work of Shakespeare's?

Later, Snow wrote that he should have chosen a less out-of-the-way topic than the Second Law of Thermodynamics, something to do with molecular biology, perhaps, but the Second Law stuck in people's minds as something which they ought to know about, sort of. There are several laws of thermodynamics and they have been formulated in several different ways but, in fairly simple terms, the first two are:

First Law of Thermodynamics: Sometimes called the Law of Conservation of Energy, this suggests that energy can be transferred from one system to another in various forms (e.g. from potential to kinetic) but that it cannot be created out of nothing or destroyed for good. Thus, the total amount of energy available in the universe remains constant.

Second Law of Thermodynamics: Heat cannot be transferred from a colder to a hotter body so processes involving energy transfer can go in only one direction, and all natural processes are irreversible. A related condition states that the entropy of an isolated system does not decrease.

The First Law is fairly easily grasped in a dumbed-down form like 'You can't get something for nothing.' Energy is transferred – for example in a car engine from a potential form (an inert tankful of petrol) to a kinetic one (the car moves) – but it cannot be created or destroyed. Rather, it is transformed. The Second Law is more tricky because it brings in the notion of entropy. Entropy is sometimes equated with disorder, but in scientific terms it is a measure of the unavailability of a system's energy to do work. In a closed system – that is, one which is not resupplied from outside – there will always be a waste/loss of energy because things don't work at 100 per cent efficiency. An old-fashioned watch which is wound by hand will work until the energy stored in the watch-spring runs down, at which point the wearer transfers some of his own energy to the spring in the act of winding the watch up again. Then the whole process starts again until the watch breaks or the watch-wearer himself winds down. At every point something is lost, that is, transformed in such a way that it cannot be retrieved. In dumbed-down form the Second Law of Thermodynamics could read: 'You can't break even.'

One of the side effects of the discovery of the Laws of Thermodynamics was to kill off the idea of perpetual motion. A perpetual-motion machine would, once started, do something useful without being supplied with energy from outside, and go on doing it forever. Like the Philosopher's stone (the hoped-for substance which would transform base metals into gold) or the elixir of life (guarantees perpetual youth/eternal life), the perpetual-motion machine preoccupied the minds of many thinkers in the days when science was still inseparable from alchemy and magic. Perpetual motion, however, flouts the laws of thermodynamics. As the economists like to say, 'There's no such thing as a free lunch.'

5

Physical

Here is a batch of laws and rules which will enable you to navigate your way through daily life, even in such extreme situations as robbing a bank, deep-sea diving or surviving in the wild. If you are looking for something tamer then you will also learn how to compute the time difference between walking a kilometre on the flat and a kilometre uphill, the proper etiquette for standing in a lift and the way your chances of dying increase year-on-year in an oddly mathematical way.

Rules of survival

Life and death

These rules about surviving in very cold conditions are organized, like many sets of instructions, by threes. In conditions of dangerously extreme cold, the first and most vital thing you should search for is shelter because according to the experts' estimation of what is going to kill you first:

1   You can survive for three hours without shelter

2   You can survive for three days without water

3   You can survive for three weeks without food

To this is sometimes added an earlier 'three' rule: You can survive for three minutes without air or in icy water.

Law of the jungle

Rudyard Kipling laid down the 'law of the jungle' in his collection of stories, *The Jungle Book* (1894) but over the years the sense of the expression has turned into something fairly distant from what Kipling originally intended it to mean. In the author's non-human world, in which the orphaned boy Mowgli is adopted by a wolf pack, the law of the jungle is a necessary code which enables the animals to survive and to live in relative peace in arduous circumstances. The Law stresses hierarchy and solidarity ('For the strength of the pack is the wolf, and the strength of the wolf is the pack') and obedience ('Luckily, the Law of the Jungle had taught him [Mowgli] to keep his temper, for in the jungle life and food depend on keeping your temper.').

But the contemporary interpretation of the law of the jungle goes against any sense of solidarity since it can be summed up as:

Every man for himself.

If any obedience is involved, it is obedience to one's own interests, and the only qualities required in this dismal and jungly world are strength and ruthlessness.

Moscow Rules

The first and generally accepted rule for spying as well as plenty of other areas of illicit or semi-licit human activity is: don't get caught. But there may be glamorous refinements to this basic tenet. In John le Carré's cold-war thriller *Smiley's People* (1980), an Estonian defector is shot on Hampstead Heath before he can have a clandestine meeting with the enigmatic and bespectacled hero, George Smiley. As he pokes around the murder site, while taking it all in and giving nothing away, Smiley muses that, on his way to the rendezvous, the dead man would have been cautious by instinct and training since he was 'playing Moscow Rules [. . .] Rules that had been invented for his survival; and the survival of his network'.

Not the least of John le Carré's achievements in the great sequence of spy novels which began with *The Spy Who Came in from the Cold* (1963) is his invention or popularization of a raft of terms such as 'lamplighters', 'scalphunters' and 'housekeepers', terms which have a special and sinister resonance in the world as seen from the Circus (the supposed headquarters of MI6 in London's Cambridge Circus). Le Carré didn't originate the word 'mole' to describe a double agent such as Kim Philby, who for years worked for the Soviets inside British Intelligence, but he certainly brought this shadowy creature into the light. The author is also the first user cited in the *Oxford English Dictionary* for the term 'honey trap' or the use of sex and seduction to get information. Despite his frequent references to them, the Moscow Rules – so named because Western agents needed to be particularly alert to survive in such a dangerous locale – don't appear to originate with le Carré. Appropriately, they seem to have coalesced out of nowhere and can be found in various formulations online and in fiction.

The list below of the Moscow Rules is as they appear in the International Spy Museum in Washington, DC, where you can even buy them in postcard form.

1   Assume nothing.

2   Never go against your gut.

3   Everyone is potentially under opposition control.

4   Don't look back; you are never completely alone.

5   Go with the flow, blend in.

6   Vary your pattern and stay within your cover.

7   Lull them into a sense of complacency.

8   Don't harass the opposition.

9   Pick the time and place for action.

10   Keep your options open.

Ryan's Rules

Frank Ryan, a car salesman, and Ernest Stickley Jr, a small-time criminal, meet when 'Stick' steals a car from Frank's Detroit lot.

Frank identifies Stick in a police line-up but deliberately wavers when it comes to giving evidence in court. Stick walks free and Ryan approaches him with a proposition. Suppose they go into business together. If they do things right, they're sure of a guaranteed income. Frank has the statistics to prove that armed robbery gives the biggest return for the least risk, and he's come up with a set of rules – 'ten rules for success and happiness' – which will keep them from getting caught.

Crime fiction fans will recognize this as an Elmore Leonard scenario. It's the starting point for one of his best novels *Swag* (1976), also published as *Ryan's Rules*. Scrawled on napkins from different cocktail bars, Frank Ryan's Rules are:

1 Always be polite on the job and say please and thank you.

2 Never say more than necessary. Less is more.

3 Never call your partner by name – unless you use a made-up name.

4 Never look suspicious or like a bum and dress well.

5 Never use your own car.

6 Never count the take in the car.

7 Never flash money in a bar or with women.

8 Never go back to an old bar or hangout once you have moved up.

9 Never tell anyone your business and never tell a junkie even your name.

10 Never associate with people known to be in crime.

Frank and Stick do go into business together and, following the rules, achieve success in their chosen field. Until things start to go wrong as, in a crime novel, they must go wrong. Perhaps Leonard was thinking of *Ryan's Rules* when, many years later, he formulated his ten rules for writing (see page 105). And Rule no. 2 here – 'Less is more' – is surely a sly reference to the saying popularized by the architect Mies van der Rohe in favour of minimalist design.

Sporting

Queensbury Rules

John Sholto Douglas, the eighth Marquess of Queensbury (1844–1900), has a significant role in both sporting and literary history. As the father of Lord Alfred Douglas, the lover of Oscar Wilde, he was so infuriated by his son's association with the great playwright that he threatened Wilde and finally left his calling card at the latter's London club with the hand-written addition 'For Oscar Wilde, posing somdomite'. Despite the misspelling, the meaning was clear and Wilde unwisely launched a libel action against Queensbury; the trial collapsed and in turn led to Wilde's prosecution on charges of homosexuality and a two-year term of imprisonment, followed by exile in Europe and his early death in 1900. Coincidentally, Queensbury died in the same year.

As a sportsman and a patron of sport, Queensbury did not write the boxing rules which bear his name – they were actually devised by John Graham Chambers, a Welsh all-rounder and sports pioneer – but he gave them his endorsement. In full, the Queensbury Rules are:

1 To be a fair stand-up boxing match in a 24-foot ring, or as near that size as practicable.

2 No wrestling or hugging allowed.

3 The rounds to be of three minutes' duration, and one minute's time between rounds.

4 If either man falls through weakness or otherwise, he must get up unassisted, 10 seconds to be allowed him to do so, the other man meanwhile to return to his corner, and when the fallen man is on his legs the round is to be resumed and continued until the three minutes have expired. If one man fails to come to the scratch[1] in the 10 seconds allowed, it shall be in the power of the referee to give his award in favour of the other man.

5 A man hanging on the ropes in a helpless state, with his toes off the ground, shall be considered down.

6 No seconds or any other person to be allowed in the ring during the rounds.

7 Should the contest be stopped by any unavoidable interference, the referee to name the time and place as

---

[1] The scratch was the line drawn in the ring to which the boxer, getting to his feet before the count of ten was finished, had to make his way in order for the encounter to resume. His ability to do so meant that he could start fighting again; hence the phrase 'up to scratch'.

soon as possible for finishing the contest; so that the match must be won and lost, unless the backers of both men agree to draw the stakes.

8   The gloves to be fair-sized boxing gloves of the best quality and new.

9   Should a glove burst, or come off, it must be replaced to the referee's satisfaction.

10 A man on one knee is considered down and if struck is entitled to the stakes.[2]

11 That no shoes or boots with spikes or springs be allowed.

12 The contest in all other respects to be governed by revised London Prize Ring Rules.

Among other things, the rules made mandatory the wearing of gloves, established the system of three-minute rounds and introduced the count of ten for a boxer who has been knocked to the ground.

Naismith's Rule

A rule of thumb which calculates approximately how long it will take to walk an uphill distance, named for the Scottish mountaineer William Naismith who formulated it in 1892. The rule is:

When walking allow 15 minutes for every kilometre of horizontal distance, plus 10 minutes for every 100 metres uphill.

---

[2] Stakes: prize money.

This may be for the fit and optimistic, and is generally reckoned the minimum time. It doesn't allow for poor terrain or sandwich-breaks or comfort stops. There have been later attempts to tweak the rule to make it more precise and there is an interesting variant about calculating downhill times. If you are walking on a gentle downhill path it will speed up your journey by about 10 minutes for every 300 metres downwards, but a very steep decline will add to your time by 10 minutes over the same distance.

The Martini Rule

On a website devoted to scuba diving, Natalie Gibb, an instructor in the United States, describes her experience of leading a group above a small shipwreck ninety feet below the surface. Noticing one of her divers lying on his side in the sand, she was far from reassured when she saw him grinning and pointing at the wreck. In her own words, she realized that in 'diver jargon, he was "narced". I ended the dive and ascended. On the surface, he told me that during the dive he thought that he was upright, and that the shipwreck, the divers, and the ocean floor were all turned on their sides as some sort of silly joke.'

To be 'narced' is to suffer from nitrogen narcosis, the potentially dangerous and disorientating effect of breathing nitrogen at a pressure which increases as the diver goes deeper. Other gases in the diver's tank, such as oxygen and carbon dioxide, may also have a narcotic effect. As suggested by the reaction of the diver in Natalie Gibb's group, this may not be an unpleasant experience. And that is part of the danger, since the mild, anaesthetized feeling of euphoria which can be induced in a 'narced' state makes the diver oblivious to risk and prone to making blunders. He may not be bothered about running out of air or feel warm even as he is actually getting chilled. In keeping with the deceptively pleasant experience, the rule-of-thumb which describes the growing dangers of going down deeper has been called the Martini Rule. This states that:

Every 10 meters (33 feet) of depth is the equivalent of drinking a martini. At 30 meters (100 feet), the depth at which Nitrogen Narcosis becomes noticeable the feeling is said to be the equivalent of having consumed 3 martinis. At 40 meters (130 feet) would be 4 martinis and so on.

Theoretical

Longfellow's Lift Rules

What's the worst thing you can do in an elevator? According to Layne Longfellow, a US psychologist, the 'ultimate egregious faux pas' is to stand facing the back wall. Experiments have shown that if someone comes into a lift and does this, then the other occupants will unconsciously crowd closer to the back even as their eyes begin to dart uneasily all over the place. Anxiety at what will happen next and shock at the breaking of a convention/taboo are at the root of this response. According to Dr Longfellow: 'If you'll do something as outrageous as to stand backwards and look at them, God knows what else you would do.'

There is a field of scientific study, known as proxemics, which examines the differing physical spaces people maintain between themselves as well as non-living objects. If you simplify the average human body, as seen from above, to a circle in the middle of an oval (for the head and shoulders) and draw a further oval round this shape, thus allowing for clothing and minimal movement or 'sway', you get an area of 2.3 square feet or just over 0.2 square metres. This cubic measure is the body-space allowance used to work out the holding capacity of New York subway carriages and also of US Army vehicles. The science of proxemics determines that the area of three square feet round someone is the 'touch zone' while seven square feet is the 'no-touch zone' and ten square feet the 'personal comfort zone'. The standard elevator measure allows for about two square feet per passenger, or well inside the touch zone. It's an intimate distance and so a potentially disturbing one.

The experience of having to share a small yet public space with people who may be strangers has given rise to 'elevator etiquette', in effect a set of generally observed but unspoken, unwritten rules – or unwritten until Dr Layne Longfellow codified them in the 1970s as follows:

1   Face forward.

2   Fold hands in front.

3   Do not make eye contact.

4   Watch the numbers.

5   Don't talk to anyone you don't know.

6   Stop talking with anyone you do know when anyone you don't know enters the elevator.

7   Avoid brushing bodies.

In a feature in the *Los Angeles Times* (20 August 1982) Longfellow amplified some of his findings, describing how the four corners of the lift are the first spaces to be taken, how people shrink themselves, hunch their shoulders and draw in their elbows as the space fills up, and how, in a really crowded elevator, people avoid having their hands clasped protectively in front of them because 'there's no telling where your knuckles might end up'.

Longfellow isn't the only person to have commented on the hidden rules of lift behaviour. Stand-up and TV host Dara O'Briain has a routine in which he describes how to freak out the other passengers by standing with your back to the door and staring them down. As O'Briain observes, 'Lifts are tremendous locations for social convention.'

Wilde's Risk Homeostasis Theory

Just as the thermostat on a radiator regulates the temperature in a room, so it's been suggested that, when it comes to the human perception of risk, a psychological mechanism constantly adjusts that perception. When circumstances change, people's risk-taking capacity fluctuates and their behaviour alters, but always with the aim of returning to a risk-acceptable norm or standard which may not even be realized on a conscious level. This process of fluctuation round a target is known as homeostasis.

Also related to risk compensation theory, risk homeostasis theory has something in common with the Law of Unexpected Consequences (see page 43 in Economics). It was laid out in the 1990s by Canadian psychologist Gerald Wilde who focused particularly on the behaviour of motorists. He argued that there was an explanation for the fact that the incorporation of various safety measures inside cars (seatbelts, airbags, overall car design) as well as outside in what he termed 'forgiving roads (collapsible lamp posts and barriers)' did not produce the drop in fatalities that might have been expected. Gerard Wilde's conclusion was that:

> People at any moment of time compare the amount of risk they perceive with their target level of risk and will adjust their behaviour in an attempt to eliminate any discrepancies between the two.

In other words, people instinctively put up with a level of risk which is comfortable to them, and fine-tune their behaviour in accordance with changes in external circumstances so that the risk-level remains at an acceptable level. On the road, the greater sense of security provided in one area (by driving a car equipped with an airbag or along a road with collapsible barriers) may be cancelled out by an increase in danger in another area, a behavioural one. Greater aggressiveness or carelessness on the driver's part may be the result because he/she is offered some guarantee against the risks of just such aggressiveness or carelessness. Similarly, better road lighting may not produce safer drivers but faster and less observant ones, while more care taken on a well-regulated stretch of road with speed cameras and so on, may be offset by more reckless driving elsewhere. Wilde also cites research showing that introduction of 'child-proof' medicine containers does not necessarily lead to a reduction in accidents because parents become less careful in their storage of the 'safe' bottles.

The theory has been criticized on the grounds of pessimism and even given alternative descriptions such as 'Wilde's Law of the conservation of Misery', referring to the old idea that misery is an irreducible constant in human life and that therefore nothing much can be done about it. But rather than guarding against the effects of careless behaviour by providing an environment which makes the motorist feel 'safe' or penalizing bad behaviour with fines and sanctions, Wilde suggests that offering incentives for good behaviour provides a more hopeful way forward.

The Gompertz's Law of Human Mortality

Do you want to know when you are going to die? Probably not. But it's a subject in which life assurance companies and institutions such as government departments have a profound interest since all sorts of decisions involving future costs depend on population growth and the related question of life expectancy. In the middle of the eighteenth century, a period when the average life expectancy in England was 37, two Church of Scotland ministers tackled the predicament of those widows and children left unprovided for by the premature death of their fellow clergy. Robert Wallace and Alexander Webster saw that dependants could be provided with annuities if ministers paid yearly premiums during their lifetimes and the money was invested. But they had to balance the books: factors included the size of the premium, the return on the investment and, most important, the average life expectancy of ministers and their wives. Drawing information from presbyteries all over Scotland, they compiled actuarial tables and, according to one estimate, got their calculations right to a single pound. Death might not have lost its sting but actuarial logic was capable of providing a salve.

Benjamin Gompertz (1779–1865) took things a stage further. He was a mathematician and actuary whose work stretched from astronomy to mortality. Largely self-taught and excluded from university because he was Jewish, Gompertz helped to draw up tables showing the position of the stars and, at around the time when he was appointed actuary to a life assurance company, he published papers illustrating the exponential pattern which governs human mortality. The Law which takes his name applies to the period between the end of puberty and around 80 years of age, and expressed in user-friendly form it says that:

Your chances of dying double every eight years.

No one has satisfactorily explained the eight-year regularity of Gompertz's law but, like the calculations of the Scottish clerics Webster and Wallace, it has proved remarkably accurate. In a post (8 July 2009) on his website, *Gravity and Levity*, which also contains a link to a handy calculator showing your chances of dying at any given age, the US physicist Brian Skinner, uses himself to illustrate Gompertz. Skinner writes: 'For me, a 25-year-old American, the probability of dying during the next year is a fairly minuscule 0.03% – about 1 in 3,000. When I'm 33 it will be about 1 in 1,500, when I'm 42 it will be about 1 in 750, and so on. By the time I reach age 100 (and I do plan on it) the probability of living to 101 will only be about 50%.'

The Gompertz Law applies only to natural death and not to sudden, violent events like being involved in a train crash or being struck by lightning (such deaths are sometimes known as examples of age-independent mortality). One partial explanation for the exponential pattern connects mortality to a falling-off in the body's immune response, a cops-and-criminals scenario in which a rogue, troublemaking cell can be 'arrested' if the police patrols of, say, the body's cancer-fighting agents are regular enough in their routine. But a small decline in the number of patrols can lead to a significant increase in the likelihood of the rogue cells establishing themselves and so an increase in the likelihood of death. It may be reassuring to octogenarians to know that, statistically, Gompertz's law doesn't seem to apply quite so rigorously after the age of 80. But by then another condition known as Old Age Frailty Syndrome will most likely have kicked in. This means that, as the body declines, a quite minor event may overwhelm the individual's ability to resist and recover. An alternative name might be the Last Straw Syndrome.

Humphrey's Law

Many of the things we do every day, from brushing our teeth to walking along the street, from reading a book to driving a car, are governed by what psychologists call automatic processing. The capacity to do these daily things has been learned, most likely over time and often with some difficulty, but once the techniques have been absorbed the tasks can be performed without much thought being given to the actual process. Anybody who's out walking doesn't think: now put the left leg forward, followed by the right leg, then the left again . . . The English psychologist George Humphrey (1880–1966) observed in *The Story of Man's Mind* (1923) that habit 'diminishes the conscious attention with which our acts are performed', and later went on to formulate the eponymous proposition/law that:

> Consciously thinking about one's performance of a task involving automatic processing impairs one's performance of it.

Examples of things which tend to go awry once you start considering how to do them include taking a golf swing or tying a tie. A more amusing formulation of the same idea appeared in a Lewis-Carroll-style poem by Katherine Craster in *Pinafore Poems* (1871). It's known as 'The Centipede's Dilemma':

> A centipede was happy – quite!
> Until a toad in fun
> Said, 'Pray, which leg goes after which?'
> And worked her mind to such a pitch,
> She lay distracted in a ditch
> Considering how to run.

6

Online

Everyone knows that the Internet is a jungle, a free-for-all where anything goes and there are no hard-and-fast rules even if there is quite an elaborate netiquette code governing personal communications. But there are some laws based on the observation of how things work online, and the best of them are listed here. And there are also a handful of scientific laws which apply to the technology. First off is one which governs the rate at which things get better or at any rate get faster.

Moore's Law

Remember those spy films and TV shows from the 1960s in which computational power was indicated by a room humming with air-conditioning and full of clunky cabinets with spinning discs and trolleys stacked high with punch cards? Then call to mind the fact that the onboard computers in the first manned moonshot had less processing power than a cell phone. Well, the astonishing increase in computing power – and the increasing rate at which it increases – has itself been computed and formulated as a law. In 1965 Gordon Moore, an electronics engineer who went on to work for Intel, wrote an article for an industry magazine titled 'Cramming More Components onto Integrated Circuits'.

Extrapolating from what was possible in the laboratory at the time he was writing, Moore predicted that as many as 65,000 components would be squeezed on a single silicon chip by 1975. This represented a doubling of capacity every year. Later Moore revised his figure to suggest a doubling of power every two years. A period of eighteen months was also suggested by an Intel colleague, and this has become the generally accepted figure even though Moore himself sticks to the two-year period. A friend of the scientist from the California Institute of Technology christened his observation Moore's Law and it can be summarized as follows:

In microprocessor development, the processing power doubles about every 18–24 months especially relative to cost or size.

Moore's Law cannot hold good forever and is predicted to collapse one day either through physical constraints, because processors will overheat once they shrink below a certain size, or because of economic constraints – that is, it will cost more and more to bring about improvements that are of decreasing significance. Whether it will be physics or economics or a combination of both that bring about that day of reckoning is uncertain but the Moorepocalypse, as it is known, keeps getting pushed further and further into the future. And that future may be determined more by Koomey's Law (see below) and less by Moore's Law.

Koomey's Law

This is closely related to Moore's Law (see above) since it deals with the exponential rise in computing speed and capacity, but it approaches the subject from a different angle: the battery rather than the chip. In 2011 a group of researchers led by Jonathan Koomey, a consulting professor of civil and environmental engineering at Stanford University, showed that the energy efficiency of computers doubles approximately every 18 months. Or, to put it the other way round, what has been referred to as Koomey's Law states that:

> At a fixed computing load, the amount of battery you need will fall by a factor of two every year and a half.

The Stanford research into the power consumption of computing devices took as its starting point the Electronic Numerical Integrator and Computer (ENIAC), which in 1946 was used to calculate artillery firing tables for the US Army and was capable of a few hundred calculations per second. Employing vacuum tubes rather than transistors, the ENIAC occupied 1,800 square feet of floor space and consumed 150 kilowatts of power. Things could only get better and they did, with energy efficiency doubling every eighteen months. And now, according to an article (September 2011) in MIT Technology Review, 'the information technology world has gradually been shifting its focus from computing capabilities to better energy efficiency, especially as people become more accustomed to using smart phones, laptops, tablets, and other battery-powered devices.'

The same MIT article points to a bright, almost infinite future. Koomey cites the well-known physicist and scientific popularizer Richard Feynman as estimating, way back in 1985, that in electrical terms the efficiency of computers could theoretically be improved by a factor of 100 billion before it hit a limit. Koomey says that since then improvements have only been of the order of 40,000 and that 'There's so far to go. It's only limited by our cleverness, not the physics.'

1 per cent rule

On the basis of the Pareto Principle (see under Economics) this is a rule of thumb about Internet use, which suggests that 90 per cent of Internet users are passive consumers:

> In any group of hundred people online, only one will be actually creating the content, while ten will be actively engaged with it by adding comments, corrections or improvements, and the other 89 will just be looking.

This is quite an old rule by Internet standards, dating back around ten years. It has been challenged on the grounds that, in the era of Facebook and Twitter, the proportion of those engaged online must have gone up. On the other hand, if the statistics are restricted to a single community or service then the rule still seems to hold good. While you may be part of the active 10 per cent for one particular thread or site, you will be part of the passive 90 per cent for many dozens of others. So rather like shoppers when the sales assistant comes up, most Internet browsers are 'just looking'. The lesson, if any, for content providers, is that a site which demands too much interaction from users is likely to be by-passed.

Ninety–Ninety Rule

Here is a paradoxical observation from programming and software engineering, which first appeared thirty years ago in a column soliciting 'bumper-sticker-sized advice' in the magazine *Communications of the ACM* (Association for Computing Machinery). Alongside the practical advice from workers in the field – 'Whenever possible, steal code' – appeared the following rule, attributed to Tom Cargill from Bell Labs and termed the Rule of Credibility even though it later became known as the Ninety–Ninety Rule:

> The first 90% of the code accounts for the first 90% of the development time. The remaining 10% of the code accounts for the other 90% of the development time.

With its total of 180 per cent the rule reflects ruefully on the fact that software development almost inevitably overruns the time scheduled for it, and that the supposedly easy bits which remain to be done once the hard part is complete often take far longer than expected. It's been observed that the Ninety–Ninety Rule has a wider application than to software development, and can describe the way many projects refuse to conform to timetables or fall victim to last-minute problems which were never foreseen.

Cunningham's Law

This was named after Ward Cunningham (b. 1949), program designer and pioneer of the wiki or website which can be edited by its users. As is usual with such laws, it was Cunningham who made the observation below but someone else – in this case, a colleague at Tektronix in the early 1980s – who gave it the title of Cunningham's Law:

> The best way to get the right answer on the Internet is not to ask a question, it's to post the wrong answer.

Hofstadter's Law

Douglas Hofstadter (b. 1945) is a cognitive scientist and author of the Pulitzer-prize-*winning Godel, Escher, Bach: An Eternal Golden Braid* (1979). In GEB Hofstadter discussed, among much else, why it was taking so long to build a chess-playing computer capable of beating a human player. One answer seemed to be that the human chess-player was at an advantage because he or she was able to fix on a specific position rather than being programmed to follow multiple possible lines of play through all their permutations, as a computer is. But the continuing difficulty of constructing that world-beating machine in the 1960s and 1970s prompted the author to come up with:

> Hofstadter's Law: It always takes longer than you expect, even when you take into account Hofstadter's Law.

Even though there are now programs capable of defeating the grandmasters, Hofstadter's Law stands as a reminder that very complex tasks will take longer than expected to achieve, even when an allowance for extra time is built into the planning – in other words, it will always take longer still. It can be seen as a variant on the Ninety–Ninety Rule (see above).

Godwin's Law

Mike Godwin is a US lawyer and editor who, in the early days of the Internet, observed how easy it was in online discussions to fall back on Hitler and the Nazis as a means of denigrating another person or point of view. And not just easy, but satisfying too. His law originally appeared in 1992 as:

> Godwin's Rule of Nazi Analogies: As a Usenet discussion grows longer, the probability of a comparison involving Nazis or Hitler approaches one.

Hitler and Nazism have long been the off-the-peg standards of ultimate evil, and the temptation to use him/it is too strong for many to resist, whatever the circumstances. You're anti-smoking? So was Hitler. A vegetarian? Just like Hitler! This sloppy, partisan use of Hitler is sometimes referred to as Reductio ad Hitlerum –

pseudo-Latin along the lines of reductio ad absurdum – and derides the idea that Hitler's like/dislike for something necessarily means that that thing is good/bad. On a more significant level, any international leader can be given a Hitlerian shading both on- and off-line. Examples range from Vladimir Putin to George W. Bush (termed 'Bushitler' by a few on the left) and the loony right-wing depiction of Barack Obama with a toothbrush moustache (on the grounds that he was reforming America's healthcare system).

Mike Godwin's Law has been sanctified by appearing in the *Oxford English Dictionary* where it is described as a 'facetious aphorism'. But in an article written for *Tablet* magazine in 2010 and reflecting on 18 years of the law's existence, Godwin said that his intention was ultimately serious: 'Although deliberately framed as if it were a law of nature or of mathematics, its purpose has always been rhetorical and pedagogical: I wanted folks who glibly compared someone else to Hitler or to Nazis to think a bit harder about the Holocaust.'

Poe's Law

Nathan Poe came up with his law during a 2005 online debate about evolution and creationism. 'Fundamentalism' was later substituted for 'creationism' to give the law wider validity:

> Without a winking smiley or other blatant display of humour, it is impossible to create a parody of fundamentalism that someone won't mistake for the real thing.

In the online world, where there is no tone of voice or body posture or hand gestures for guidance, it's not always easy to tell whether someone is being serious or ironic. This opens the gates to mischief. Websites which feature genuinely held but extreme opinions may prompt satirical responses, in pretended agreement. Conversely, an ironical web page may be taken at face value, which is a reflection either on the average browser or the fact that the web, though fertile ground for everything else, is not very conducive to irony. To take just one example: the site for the Landover Baptist Church – 'guaranteeing Salvation since 1620!' – may look kosher at first glimpse, but a brief examination of its contents (such as the profile of Pastor Bubba T. Gatlin who 'shot a man dead at point blank range in 1948 for rejecting the Lord Jesus Christ') quickly reveals its pleasing satirical intent.

The knack of missing irony long predates the online world, even if the plethora of bloggers, mischief makers and plain nutters out there makes the question 'Are you being serious?' ever harder to answer. There were undoubtedly readers who took at face value, even if only for a moment, the savage plan outlined by Jonathan Swift in his pamphlet *A Modest Proposal* (1729), that the children of the poor should be fattened to feed the rich, so relieving their parents of a financial burden and 'making them beneficial to the public'. Swift includes serving suggestions – 'A Child will make two Dishes at an Entertainment for Friends; and when the Family dines alone, the fore or hind Quarter will make a reasonable Dish' – and keeps a resolute, dead-pan face throughout. An ideal candidate for Poe's Law.

Rule 34

This arbitrarily numbered law is the caption to a webcomic cartoon drawn in 2003 by Peter Morley-Souter. In the picture a geeky teen looks dumbfounded at his desktop screen. We can't see what he's looking at. The speech bubble from his mouth says 'Calvin and Hobbes?' Above the drawing is the caption:

Rule 34: There is porn of it. No exceptions.

And below is the tag line 'The Internet, raping your childhood since 1996.' Morley-Souter was registering his shock, in a cool kind of way, at seeing Calvin and Hobbes, children's cartoon characters, engaging in sex. Rule 34[1] has been restated in various minor ways, such as 'If it exists, there is Internet porn of it', all of them pointing to the phenomenal boost which the Internet has given to pornography and to the fact that there is no sexual nook or cranny too small or too weird not to be catered for by someone, somehow, somewhere. As the US comedian Richard Jeni put it: 'The Web brings people together because no matter what kind of a twisted sexual mutant you happen to be, you've got millions of pals out there. Type in "Find people that have sex with goats that are on fire" and the computer will say, "Specify type of goat".'

---

[1] Rule 34 should not be confused, by inversion, with Rule 43 which in British jails provided for the segregation of prisoners, usually sex offenders, for their own safety or for the sake of 'good order and discipline'. (It is now Prison Service Rule 45.)

Lewis's Law

Anyone who ventures into the below-the-line comments in blogs and articles knows that the experience can be akin to lifting up a large stone in the garden and seeing some very odd, often unpleasant forms of life crawling beneath. That may even be the situation after the comments have been filtered and the most outrageous remarks removed from the thread by a moderator. In 2014 the *Chicago Sun-Times* temporarily closed the comment function that accompanies their features because the paper's staff had grown increasingly disillusioned with negative and critical comments below the line.

Women who blog or whose articles appear online have long been familiar with the abuse than can come with daring to have an opinion and express it. In an article in November 2011 in the *New Statesman* ('"You should have your tongue ripped out": the reality of sexist abuse online'), Helen Lewis described the sheer volume of sexual abuse faced by women online as 'the Internet's festering sore' and proved the point with stories from nine women bloggers who had been on the receiving end of everything from insults about their physical appearance to rape and death threats. As one said: 'Being a woman on the internet seemed to be enough to anger people, regardless of what you were writing.'

In August 2012 Helen Lewis, who is now deputy editor on the *Statesman*, posted a comment on Twitter which she defined as Lewis's Law. It was subsequently picked up and quoted elsewhere and has gained some traction in the world of Internet laws, a world which is still almost entirely male-dominated. Lewis's Law states:

The comments on any article about feminism justify feminism.

7

Life and work

Daily life is the cause, excuse or provocation for dozens of rules and observations, many of them of the Murphy's Law variety. But it is the frustrations of work which offer a particularly rich crop, almost every one of them focusing on other people's shortcomings, specially those in authority.

Office life and bureaucracy

Parkinson's Law

It all started with an unattributed article in *The Economist* in November 1955. The author had a point to make and he used the illustration of an 'elderly lady of leisure' who is capable of spending a whole day in the project of sending a postcard to her niece in Bognor Regis. She takes so long because she first has to find the postcard, then her glasses, then the address, before getting down to write the thing and deciding whether she needs to take an umbrella on her trip to the pillar-box. The anonymous author concluded that:

> Work expands so as to fill the time available for its completion.

The man behind *The Economist* article was Cyril Northcote Parkinson (1909–93), who has some claim to be the grandfather of amateur law-making. In the words of Paul Dickson in *The Official Rules* (1978) it was Parkinson who 'more than anyone else helped break the stranglehold of the pure sciences and mathematics on immutable laws, principles and effects. He paved the way for others.'

When he coined the famous law of 'work expands…', Parkinson was a university lecturer in Malaya. The article was a response to a Royal Commission report on the Civil Service, and took up the usual satirical approach that, like other large organizations, the Service was both over-staffed and underemployed. But Parkinson did it with a sureness of touch and a cod-scientific seriousness, complete with charts and equations, which meant that his message hit home. With a lifelong interest in the navy – he was later to write Hornblower-style sea stories – Parkinson naturally turned to Admiralty statistics and showed that for the period 1914–28 there had been an increase of over 75 per cent in staff at Whitehall but a reduction of a third in the number of serving men (and two-thirds in the total of ships). By 1954 the Admiralty staff had quadrupled. Concluding that there was an inexorable law behind such bureaucratic growth, which averaged 5–7 per cent a year, Parkinson said that the '*officials would have multiplied at the same rate had there been no actual seamen at all*' (his italics). The increase he put down to two factors: (1) an official wants to multiply subordinates, not rivals; (2) officials make work for each other.

Parkinson's Law, the book launched on the back of the article, was a best-seller and Parkinson became an academic celebrity and Channel Island tax exile. He also created Parkinson's Law of Triviality, which tells us that 'the time spent on any item will be in inverse proportion to its cost and importance.' Parkinson illustrated this with the example of an executive board discussing two new projects, the construction of an atomic reactor and the building of a new bike shed. (Would these occur on the same agenda? Yes, for the purposes of this example.) The reactor question will be decided, says Parkinson, in two-and-a-half minutes because it's a highly complex issue outside almost everyone's experience, and therefore few people will dare to venture a view. Everyone, however, can have a view on a bike shed and, being keen to speak up and show their expertise (especially since they've kept quiet about the reactor), they will happily chat for forty-five minutes before sitting back with a sense of accomplishment because they have saved £50 with their deliberations.

(See also the Dilbert Principle and the Peter Principle.)

The Dilbert Principle

There aren't that many cartoon strips which take the workplace as a setting; in Britain, only the now-defunct 'Bristow' in the *Evening Standard* and the *Telegraph*'s high-finance 'Alex' spring to mind. In the United States the Dilbert strip, produced by cartoonist Scott Adams, has been satirizing office life and mid-level management since 1989. In a February 1995 strip Adams has his talking-dog character explain leadership. Leaders, says Dogbert, are meeting-loving morons with tiny brains and large bladders. Their ability to hold coffee and their imperviousness to logic are perceived as leadership qualities so that eventually they are promoted. Thus, Dogbert concludes, 'leadership is nature's way of removing morons from the productive flow.'

The Dilbert Principle, which has a deliberate touch of paradox, is usually summarized as the process by which:

> Companies routinely promote their least able employees to management positions to limit the harm they can cause.

Scott Adams enlarged on this and other ideas in his best-selling *The Dilbert Principle* (1996). According to this theory, promotion becomes not a reward but a way of removing useless or minimally competent people from actual, meaningful work. Adams later commented: 'You want them [the least smart people] ordering the doughnuts and yelling at people for not doing their assignments – you know, the easy work. Your heart surgeons and your computer programmers – your smart people – aren't in management.'

(See also Parkinson's Law and the Peter Principle.)

The Peter Principle

This is often seen as connected to the Dilbert Principle since it relates to people's incompetence and their promotion in the workplace. However, Peter's Principle has a different emphasis and could even be seen as contradictory to Dilbert's.[1] Laurence J. Peter (1919–90) was a Canadian-born educationalist working in the United States who first put forward his Principle in the *Oakland Tribune* newspaper and then, with fellow-Canadian Raymond Hull, wrote *The Peter Principle: Why Things Always Go Wrong* (1969). Put simply, the Peter Principle states that:

> In an organizational hierarchy, all employees will rise or be promoted to their level of incompetence.

Dr Peter also expressed his principle along the proverbial lines of 'the cream rises until it sours'. The underlying idea is that employees are selected for promotion on the basis of ability in their current position, rather than their future one. This may be especially the case when an individual in a specialist role (like an engineer) is considered for a quite different kind of job requiring quite different skills (like a managerial one). According to Peter, it is only when employees reach a level at which they show manifest incompetence that their chances of further promotion slip away. The distinction between Peter and Dilbert is clearest here, since Peter maintains that people rise up because of their competence (in a previous post) while Dilbert holds that promotion is the result of incompetence (in a present post).

---

[1] Like Dilbert, the Peter Principle was also the title and theme of a cartoon series when in 1985 Laurence Peter was commissioned to provide the gags and speech bubbles for a sequence of syndicated cartoons (sample: one student to another outside a counsellor's office: 'Who would take career advice from someone who ended up as a guidance counselor?'). Although the ironies of official incompetence are a traditional source of humour, the series never really took off.

A notable example of the Peter Principle in operation was the appointment by President George W. Bush of his friend Michael D. Brown to head the Federal Emergency Management Agency (FEMA). After Hurricane Katrina struck New Orleans in 2005, FEMA and Brown in particular were accused of bungling incompetence in their response. Despite Bush's misplaced praise – 'Brownie, you're doing a heck of a job' – Brown eventually asked to be relieved of his position with the plaintive words 'Can I quit now?' Brown's original appointment came about not just because of his friendship with the president but because of his proven expertise in another role: he had served as the commissioner of judges for the International Arabian Horse Federation. Unfortunately the gap between this post and a quite different one requiring him to handle a major national emergency was too wide for him to bridge.

(See also Parkinson's Law and the Dilbert Principle.)

Rothbard's Law

Murray Rothbard (1926–95) was an American economist and academic, out of the Austrian or Chicago School of economic thinking, whose free-market theories and anti-government creed have delivered so much to so few in the last forty years. Rothbard's ideas were on the crazed edge of libertarian thinking, for example suggesting that parents had the right not to feed or clothe their children, or giving permission to the police to torture some suspects, such as murderers, on the grounds that they are only dealing out part of what the suspect deserves. After that, it's a relief to read that if the suspect is found not guilty then the police themselves will end up in the dock for criminal assault. Perhaps Rothbard's ideas were a life-long exercise in irony. Certainly there is a mischievous quality about Rothbard's Law, which seems to be directed at academic specialisms but also has a wider application:

People tend to specialize in what they are worst at.

Sayre's Law

Any fan of Colin Dexter's novels featuring the grumpy detective Inspector Morse or of the long-running TV series simply called *Morse* and starring John Thaw will know that Oxford is one of the murder capitals of the world, with a mortality rate only outdone in England by the (fortunately fictional) county of Midsomer. Yet perhaps no one should be so surprised that a high-powered intellectual centre, home to a famous university, is also a nest of murderous intrigue and passion.

The notion that academic disputes are especially bitter has been around for a long time. Dr Johnson, in the introduction to his edition of Shakespeare's plays, observed that there is no animosity like that which festers among critics and commentators, despite the fact that the 'subjects to be discussed by him are of very small importance; they involve neither property nor liberty; nor favour the interest of sect or party'.

It seems to have been Wallace Sayre (1905–72), a professor of political science at Columbia University, who laid down the law that:

Academic politics is the most vicious and bitter form of politics, because the stakes are so low.

An observation which is sometimes modified as below, and in a way which most of us would say applies well beyond academia:

> In any dispute the intensity of feeling is inversely proportional to the value of the stakes at issue.

The bitter intensity of differences of religious opinion among sectarians and scholars gave rise to the expression 'odium theologicum', first noted in 1734 and described as 'the intemperate zeal of Divines'. The best-known spin-off is 'odium academicum', but Sayre's Law goes one further by stressing not just the hatred of the dispute but the pettiness of the cause.

Pournelle's Law

Jerry Pournelle (b. 1933) is a US sci-fi writer and theorist who has worked with Larry Niven, among other literary collaborators (see Niven's Law). Like other sci-fi writers such as Robert Heinlein, Pournelle is known for his robustly libertarian and right-wing stance. Pournelle's iron law of bureaucracy is typical of his outlook.

> In any bureaucracy, the people devoted to the benefit of the bureaucracy itself always get in control, and those dedicated to the goals the bureaucracy is supposed to accomplish have less and less influence, and sometimes are eliminated entirely.

Pournelle enlarged on this with the example of those teachers who work hard to do their best for children contrasted with those teaching union representatives who work solely to protect any member regardless of his or her competence.

Life theories

The Helsinki Bus Station Theory

In this book of laws, rules and principles I have generally avoided the ones which give advice on how to get on in life, love and work. You know the kind of thing, self-help manuals which appear under titles such as 'The Six Rules of Effective Communication' or 'Think like an Aztec'. Although the The Helsinki Bus Station Theory falls into the life-guidance category, it's worth citing not so much because the advice may be good – and it probably is good advice – but because of the idiosyncratic, eye-catching way it is formulated. In four short words, the Helsinki Bus Station Theory tells us that if there's one thing we must do in life it is to:

Stay on the bus.

It was proposed by the Finnish photographer Arno Minkkinen in a commencement speech delivered at the New England School of Photography in June 2004. Minkkinen introduced his student audience to an allegory involving the Bus Station in Helsinki, a terminus with two dozen platforms, each one a departure point for several bus lines, say numbers 21, 71, 58, 33 and 19. So you get on one of the buses and discover that the line you're on is used by those other differently numbered buses (21, 71, etc.) for a kilometre or two before the routes begin to diverge. There are several stops on these shared kilometres. Minkkinen suggests that each stop might represent, metaphorically, a single year in the life of a young professional photographer who has committed to a particular activity, for example platinum studies of nudes. After three stops/years, you take the 'work on the nude to the Museum of Fine Arts Boston and the curator asks if you are familiar with the nudes of Irving Penn. His bus, 71, was on the same line. Or you take them to a gallery in Paris and are reminded to check out Bill Brandt, bus 58, and so on.'

Alarmed and dismayed at the realization that everything you're doing has been done before, and probably been done better too, you go back to the bus-station taking a cab – because life is short – and catch another bus from another platform. A different route, a different photographic line, another three stops/years, another display of your work. And once again comes the same comment from the curators, critics and gallery owners: you must surely be familiar with the work of X, Y, Z (all well-known), because you're doing what they are doing. Yet another cab back to the bus-station, another platform, another route. With the same short-term result. You'll never get anywhere. But the real answer, says Minkkinen is 'simple. Stay on the bus. Stay on the fucking bus'.

Persistence pays is part of the point of the allegory, which was also developed by Oliver Burkeman in one of his regular *Guardian* features titled 'This column will change your life' (23 February 2013). In the same way as the bus routes out of Helsinki Station eventually diverge, so too will your chosen artistic line eventually part company from those of the others who have gone before you. You will develop a vision which will be individual and, in the long run, your work will be viewed as a totality in which the early pieces have their own validity rather than being seen as imitations of someone else's work.

The Van Halen Principle

In the pomp of their 1980s heyday, the US rock band Van Halen sent out 'contract riders' to the venues where they were going to perform. These shopping lists were extensive and specific, listing all the amenities, goodies and frills to be provided for the band. So, among much else, the 1982 World Tour rider contained demands for: four cases of Schlitz Malt Liquor and one pint of Southern Comfort, as well as herrings in sour cream, celery, twelve fresh lemons (with knife and cutting board) and one large tube of K-Y jelly. In the 'munchies' section comes the instruction to provide M&Ms, qualified with the bizarre warning that there should be 'absolutely no brown ones'. So some unfortunate gopher must have had the task of weeding out the brown ones from a pile of multicoloured M&Ms.

This famous exclusion clause has passed into history as an example of neurotic rock-star excess and narcissism. Yet the no-brown-M&Ms rider was far from being as stupid as it appeared. In the words of singer David Lee Roth: 'Van Halen was the first to take 850 par lamp lights – huge lights – around the country. At the time, it was the biggest production ever.' If venues weren't properly prepared because the organizers hadn't taken note of all the other band requirements – the more serious ones – then the delays, costs and even dangers started to multiply. This was the thinking behind the M&M test. 'If I came backstage and I saw brown M&M's on the catering table', said Roth, 'it guaranteed the promoter had not read the contract rider, and we had to do a serious line check.'

In an article for the *Washington Post* of 2 May 2013, the blogger and journalist Ezra Klein cited the no-brown-M&Ms rider as an illustration of what he called the Van Halen Principle. As he defined it:

> Tales of someone doing something unbelievably stupid or selfish or irrational are often just stories you don't yet understand.

Ezra Klein gave various examples from the world of Washington politics, including one about a Republican politician who sniped at scientific research which involved putting shrimp on treadmills. By no means frivolous or extravagant, the shrimp-on-a-treadmill experiment was meant to find out whether shrimp are being weakened by oceanic bacteria, something which, if proved, could have a disastrous effect on the food chain. A politician, by indulging in the usual government-waste platitudes and ignoring the Van Halen Principle, makes an assumption of stupidity and fails to look at the whole picture. In the same way, in the United Kingdom, there is a widespread myth that laws and regulations emanating from the European Union – 'Brussels' in right-wing shorthand – must be pointless, intrusive, absurd and so on, when there is usually a good reason behind them. The Van Halen Principle is an implicit appeal not to rush to judgement.

The Jardin Principle

The principle which goes by the name of Occam's Razor (see below) tells us that when examining a problem we shouldn't complicate things unnecessarily. If in doubt, plump for the simple answer. Sutton's Law (see below also) has a similar message. But complication, especially if it goes under the name of complexity, has its own appeal and we may feel that the simple answer is actually a simplistic one. Unless it's not simplistic after all but so simple as to be truly profound.

Rob Eastaway, maths guru and author of *Why Do Buses Come in Threes?: The Hidden Maths of Everyday Life*, navigated a path through these slippery concepts and, in 1990, invented the Jardin Principle, after the French word for garden and in homage to the Peter Sellers's film *Being There*, about a simple gardener who becomes US President. In Eastaway's formulation, when you are getting to grips with a subject or a process your understanding goes through three stages:

To start with, the way that you see and describe a system will be simplistic i.e. over-simplified, then it will become complicated but ultimately it will become simple again.

An alternative way to describe this progress is from the obvious to the sophisticated and finally to the profound. In support of Jardin, Rob Eastaway cites Steve Jobs's widely quoted comments:

When you start looking at a problem and it seems really simple, you don't really understand the complexity of the problem. Then you get into the problem, and you see that it's really complicated, and you come up with all these convoluted solutions. That's sort of the middle, and that's where most people stop. But the really great person will keep on going and find the key, the underlying principle of the problem – and come up with an elegant, really beautiful solution that works.

It helps that the Jardin Principle conforms to the rule of three, and that it fits the pattern of countless narratives in which a confident starter meets inevitable obstacles along the way. The obstacles produce discouragement, self-questioning and even despair but they lead to growth and will, eventually and inevitably, be overcome until a resolution is reached or a destination arrived at. The Jardin Principle is also echoed in the lives of some artists whose work, from straightforward beginnings, goes through stages that move from the complex to an ultimate simplicity.

Sutton's Law

A superb scene in the political film thriller, *All the President's Men* (1976), has Robert Redford, playing the part of reporter Bob Woodward, nervously approaching a secret meeting with Deep Throat, his inside informant on the scandal that began with a small-time burglary in the Watergate building in Washington and ended in the resignation of President Nixon. The film scene is set in an underground car park, full of echoes, shadows and paranoia. Redford/Woodward is frustrated that the investigation into corruption in Nixon's administration is getting nowhere. Deep

Throat's advice to him is simple: 'Follow the money',[2] the chain of secret payments that were passed from hand to hand in the increasingly rotten circle round the president. In a world which is full of doubt and duplicity, money and the path it forges for itself are the obvious things to hold on to, perhaps the only things.

Willie Sutton (1901–80) was an accomplished US bank robber, who in his long career was estimated to have netted $2 million even if it came at the cost of spending more than half his adult life in prison. In response to a reporter who asked why he robbed banks, Sutton is supposed to have said, 'Because that's where the money is.' In fact, this smart/obvious reply seems to have been a journalist's invention. Even though the phrase became identified with him, Sutton claimed in his autobiography, titled 'Where the Money Was' and published towards the end of his life, that he robbed banks not so much for financial gain but because 'I enjoyed it. I loved it.' The meaning of Sutton's Law, however, is nothing to do with bank-robbery, and only indirectly connected with money. Rather it states that:

When diagnosing a problem, one should first consider the obvious.

Sutton's Law is used in medicine, social sciences and other fields. It suggests that a doctor or researcher should focus on

---

[2] An older and more romantic counterpart to 'Follow the money' and another example of looking for the obvious is the French expression *Cherchez la femme*, literally 'Look for the woman', if you are searching for a reason why a man is behaving oddly or out of character. It was coined by the nineteenth-century novelist Alexandre Dumas.

the obvious causes and answers to a problem before turning to more recondite solutions. This is likely to be a more productive approach as well as a more cost-effective one. The Law was allegedly created by George Dock who, as a visiting professor at Yale, was presented with an 'interesting' patient – that is, one whose problem could not be diagnosed – who had been subject to a variety of tests which failed to resolve the problem. Dock considered that a liver biopsy was the obvious (but untried) course, asking 'Why don't you follow Sutton's Law?', and telling the story of the bank-robber's apocryphal reply to the reporter. In other words, first use your common sense.

Sutton's Law is a variant on the principle known as Occam's razor, after the medieval philosopher William of Ockham, who frequently invoked the 'law of parsimony'. Put simply, this means that in looking for an explanation, one should favour the least complicated answer or, to put it more formally, that 'no more entities, causes, or forces than necessary should be invoked in explaining a set of facts or observations' (OED). And there is a variant on Occam's razor known as Hanlon's Razor which states that one should 'never attribute to malice that which is adequately explained by stupidity'. The saying has been attributed not only to Robert J. Hanlon but also to the sci-fi writer Robert Heinlein. This one also has echoes of Grey's Law: 'Any sufficiently advanced incompetence is indistinguishable from malice' (see under Clarke's Law).

(See also cock-up theory.)

The 10,000 hour rule

Malcolm Gladwell (b. 1963), the professional out-of-the-box thinker, popularized the 10,000 hour rule in his book *Outliers* (2008). He argued that one of the keys to great achievement in any area of life is a great investment of time, and came up with the rule that:

> Roughly 10,000 hours of practice are necessary to achieve mastery in a field.

Gladwell cited several examples, including Bill Gates, who was obsessed with computer programming from the late 1960s and long before founding Microsoft, as well as the Beatles, who served a lengthy apprenticeship while an unknown band in the Hamburg clubs by playing lengthy sessions every night of the week. Gladwell later commented that his rule had been misinterpreted to suggest that intensive, lengthy practice was, in itself, enough for success. Not so, he said, innate talent is necessary, coupled with intensive practice which will usually begin early in life. Also, some skills especially in sports – throwing darts comes to mind – are intrinsically easier to acquire than other skills, such as brain surgery, and therefore do not fall under the 10,000 hour rule.

Nelson Algren's Three Rules of Life

US writer Nelson Algren's best-known novels are *The Man with the Golden Arm* (1949) and *A Walk on the Wild Side* (1956), later used by Lou Reed as a song title and also the source of the rules below. In his fiction Algren identified with the American underclass, with drop-outs and has-beens, and his three warnings are part of a longer list of instructions from an old hand to a younger man who's thinking about 'going into crime serious'. The rules are:

1   Never play cards with a man called Doc.

2   Never eat at a place called Mom's.

3   And never sleep with a woman whose troubles are worse than your own.

Grumpy old laws

Hutber's Law

There is a small category of laws which are close to being aphorisms and which express a grumpiness or cynicism that is generally identified with age, experience, world-weariness and so on. Not surprisingly, these tend to find themselves at home in conservative circles and right-leaning outlets. Patrick Hutber was the city editor of the *Sunday Telegraph*. Famous for his scoops, he was also known for his reckless driving. He died in 1980 after crashing his sports car but enjoys a kind of posthumous life in the eponymous Hutber's Law, which states that:

Improvement means deterioration.

Hutber's Law is useful when griping about modern life but it has a natural fit with financial journalism and commentary, as in this representative quote from the *Daily Telegraph*: 'Now, though, the new, high-speed Royal Mail has offered to deliver it by 7am, for an extra annual payment of £2,218 – but there's no guarantee that it will be ready by then. [. . .] It is, as some readers will instantly recognise, a perfect example of Hutber's Law – Improvement means deterioration.'

Also fitting in this category is a law or observation made by the novelist Kingsley Amis. Writing in *Encounter* magazine in 1960 on the planned expansion in higher education, Amis predicted: 'More will mean worse.' This soon became simplified in more memorable form as:

More means worse.

Although Kingsley Amis had a justified reputation as a crusty, anti-liberal figure in his later years – a reputation that he played up to – he was only 38 when he promulgated the 'More means worse' rule. As with Hutber's Law, the observation has been applied to many areas apart from higher education. These aphoristic laws are straightforward in their irony: a word (improvement, more) leading one to expect something positive is equated with its opposite (deterioration, worse). Their structure echoes a well-known saying of the architect Mies van der Rohe who advocated minimalism in design and was famous for his pronouncement: 'Less is more.' The nineteenth-century poet Robert Browning used the same paradoxical phrase in his poem 'Andrea del Sarto'.

Herblock's Law

Herblock was the signature name of the US political cartoonist Herbert Lawrence Block (1909–2001). A liberal artist, he is usually credited with the invention of the term 'McCarthyism', to describe the witch-hunt conducted by Senator Joe McCarthy in the early 1950s to root out supposed communist sympathizers in various American institutions. When the manufacturers stopped making a certain kind of carbon drawing-stick that he liked using for his creations, he coined what has become known as Herblock's Law:

If it's good they'll stop making it.

Spencer's Law

As a counterpart to Hutber's and Amis's laws of deterioration (see above), Spencer's Law is a reminder that things are rarely, if ever, as bad as they seem. Like many eponymous laws, the attribution is retrospective, and in this case it was made as recently as 2001 by academic Stephen Davies to the Victorian sociologist Herbert Spencer (1820–1903). The Law states:

The degree of public concern and anxiety about a social problem or phenomenon varies inversely as to its real or actual incidence.

Or, as Spencer expressed it in an essay published in 1891: 'the more things improve the louder become the exclamations about their badness.' As examples, Herbert Spencer took subjects which were of widespread public concern at the time (as they still are now), such as consumption of drink or educational standards or poverty, despite the fact that in all these areas the later Victorian period showed a marked improvement over the early nineteenth century. Stephen Davies, who is sceptical of the value of government intervention in bringing about social improvement, suggests several reasons why people exaggerate contemporary problems and always have done. A lack of historical perspective and knowledge means that we can't properly compare the past with the present. The very fact that things are generally improving means that we tend to notice those anomalous instances where there is no change; if the majority of the population is poor or ill-educated, the problem will not be so obvious. And the sheer public appetite for bad news and hand-wringing anguish shouldn't be underestimated, either. Part of us likes to hear that things ain't what they used to be.

Tuchman's Law

This is connected to Spencer's Law, above, in that it suggests that there is a gap between the way things appear and the reality, but a gap that is actually positive because the reality is better than the report. Barbara Tuchman (1912–89) was an American historian whose best-known and most popular books, *The Guns of August* (1962) and *A Distant Mirror* (1978), deal respectively with the outbreak of World War I and, in the words of her subtitle, the 'calamitous fourteenth century'. In the introduction to *A Distant Mirror* the author mentions various problems lying in wait for historians and makes an observation which she terms Tuchman's Law:

> The fact of being reported multiplies the apparent extent of any deplorable development by five- to tenfold (or any figure the reader would care to supply).

She explains that the very act of recording disastrous events can cause them to seem continuous and ubiquitous, whereas in reality they are scattered in time and space. As Barbara Tuchman says dryly: 'After absorbing the news of today, one expects to face a world consisting entirely of strikes, crimes, power failures, broken water mains, stalled trains, school shutdowns, muggers, drug addicts, neo-Nazis and rapists. The fact is that one can come home in the evening – on a lucky day – without having encountered more than one or two of these phenomena.'

W. H. Auden makes much the same point about dramatic events and daily life in his poem 'Musee de Beaux Arts', which focuses on a Brueghel picture depicting the mythical figure of Icarus plunging into the sea after his waxen wings melt because he flew too close to the sun. Brueghel reduces Icarus to a tiny pair of legs about to be submerged at the edge of the picture. In the foreground a ploughman ploughs on, oblivious. In the middle ground a ship sails by, regardless. According to Auden, however sensational an event, it will always take place 'While someone else is eating or opening a window or just walking dully along.' All illustrations of Tuchman's Law.

Segal's Law

This doesn't seem to have originated with a man called Segal, and in any case his name was actually Lee Segall, an advertising and broadcasting executive in Dallas before and after World War II. Later he was credited with the saying which has become known as Segal's Law:

> It's possible to possess too much. A man with one watch knows what time it is; a man with two watches is never sure.

In fact it seems that Lee Segall was using an older and unattributed observation, the general gist of which is that having too much information can lead to confusion, particularly when one has to make a decision. Using the example of the watches, this applies if the two give different times and the wearer has to choose which one is right.

Cohn's Law

I haven't been able to find out who Cohn was, or even his (or her) first name. But the law associated with an individual called Cohn goes back to at least the early 1970s and it seems particularly apt in the age of the tweet and the twitter. Cohn's Law states that:

> The more time you spend in reporting on what you are doing, the less time you have to do anything. Stability is achieved when you spend all your time doing nothing but reporting on the nothing you are doing.

Mencken's Law

The American journalist, satirist and essayist, H. L. Mencken (1880–1956) would have plenty of material to work on in the current state of his native country where great swathes of the population believe in creationism and the literal truth of the Bible. Mencken covered the famous 1926 'monkey trial' in Tennessee, writing columns mocking the anti-evolution side, and in the same year he deliberately got himself arrested in Boston over the publication of a supposedly obscene story in a magazine he edited. He took an aggressive attitude to censorship and regularly defended novelists and others accused of 'smut'. His dictionary-style definition of puritanism says it all: 'The haunting fear that someone, somewhere, may be happy.'

Mencken's first journalistic job was as a reporter in Baltimore and in a memoir titled 'Drill for a Rookie', he describes attending murder scenes, executions and other sensational events (it was Mencken who made the famous observation: 'Nobody ever went broke underestimating the taste of the American public'). During a city campaign against immorality, he found himself called on to testify, unwillingly, to having seen in a 'bawdy dance-hall' two detectives who must have been aware of the kind of things which were going on there. He knew that they were technically guilty but he qualified his testimony before the police board with so many ifs and buts that the 'poor flatfeet' were acquitted. From that moment on, Mencken decided his position on such moral crusades:

I made up my mind at once that my true and natural allegiance was to the Devil's party, and it has been my firm belief ever since that all persons who devote themselves to forcing virtue on their fellow men deserve nothing better than kicks in the pants. Years later I put that belief into a proposition which I ventured to call Mencken's Law, to wit:

Whenever A annoys or injures B on the pretense of saving or improving X, A is a scoundrel.

The moral theologians, unhappily, have paid no heed to this contribution to their science, and so Mencken's Law must wait for recognition until the dawn of a more enlightened age.

Fetridge's Law

If you go to the website for the picturesque tourist attraction that is the Mission San Juan Capistrano in California's Orange County, you will learn the story of the swallows. Every year on 19 March, St Joseph's Day, these birds return to the ruined church in the Mission to begin rebuilding their mud nests. Then, after enjoying the Californian summer, on 23 October, St John's Day, the swallows depart for their winter home in Argentina. So predicable is the swallows' arrival and departure that you could set, if not a clock, then a calendar by them. Back in 1937 Claude Fetridge, a radio engineer, had the idea of broadcasting, live, the noise of their fluttering wings during their mass October 23rd leave-taking. His company spent time and money setting up outside-broadcasting equipment to capture the moment. Unfortunately the waiting American public – broadcasting pleasures must have been simpler in those days – never got the chance to hear the departing swallows since the birds had already left the Mission, on the previous day. This led to the formulation of Fetridge's Law, which aficionados will recognize as a variant of Murphy's (see below):

Important things that are supposed to happen do not happen, especially when people are looking.

Murphy's Law

There is no agreement over the source for this famous law of human life, endeavour and frustration, which can be expressed in various forms all tending to the same wry lesson:

If anything can go wrong, it will.

So wide-ranging is this law, so universal is the human experience of discovering that things are not working out quite as they should, and especially if a lot hinges on the result, it is not surprising that Murphy's Law pops up in many guises. In this book, Fetridge's Law, Hofstadter's Law, Muphry's Law, the Law of Unintended Consequences, and others, could all be grouped under Murphy's leaky umbrella.

There is not even a consensus as to whether there was ever a Murphy to give his name to the law in the first place. One well-documented account does have a Captain Edward Murphy christening the law in the late 1940s during US Air Force tests on the gravitational effects on pilots of rapid deceleration. When gauges measuring the experiments were found to have been wired the wrong way round by his assistant, resulting in a zero reading, Murphy is supposed to have made an observation along the lines that if one way of doing a job will end in disaster then someone, sooner or later, will do it that way. On the other hand, and according to John Glenn, the first American to orbit the earth, Murphy never existed. Rather, he was 'a fictitious character who appeared in a series of educational cartoons put out by the US Navy [. . .] a careless, all-thumbs mechanic who was prone to make such mistakes as installing a propellor backwards.' If this is so, Murphy's Law would seem to be more 'Don't do as I do', a warning to be vigilant, rather than a wry comment on human activity.

Whoever Murphy was, or whether he even existed, the idea that his law embodies – that where things can go wrong, they will – must be as old as humanity itself.

Sod's Law, often cited as being the same as Murphy's, belongs to British rather than American English and is, surprisingly, of quite recent date (first seen in print in 1970). It is sometimes claimed that Sod's Law applies to accidents of fate or fortune, often quite minor ones, like rain falling on bank holidays or the doorbell ringing as you get in the shower. By contrast, Murphy's Law applies more to human miscalculation, incompetence and fallibility.

. . . and finally

Rafferty's Rules

There is some doubt about the etymological origins of this Australian expression, first noted at the beginning of the twentieth century. 'Rafferty' may refer to a long-ago Irish clan settled down under, and renowned for its bad behaviour and lawlessness, or the word may be an alteration of 'raffertory', itself a variant on refractory (=obstinate, rebellious). Whatever their origin, Rafferty's Rules characterize a state of anarchy and can be summed up as follows:

There are no rules.

Rafferty's Rules, an expression which has never crossed over into British English, is still used in Australia and was the title of a TV drama series shown there in the 1980s. An approximate, if dated, English equivalent is the phrase 'Liberty Hall', as employed by Oliver Goldsmith in his play *She Stoops to Conquer* (1773): 'This is Liberty-hall, gentlemen. You may do just as you please.'

8

Laws of the land

The other sections of this book have been about laws which aren't actually laws in a legal sense, as well as rules which don't have to observed (though you may come a cropper if you ignore them), and about scientific principles which are there to be discovered and analysed but which already exist on some pre-human level. Finally, and by contrast, here is a selection of real man-made laws, which are included here for their historical or curiosity value.

Salic Law

Salic Law was the legal code originally written in Latin (Lex Salica) and governing the Salian Franks, the Germanic confederation of tribes which became increasingly dominant in Western Europe from the early Middle Ages and controlled the territory that eventually became France (the word derives from Francia, i.e.

the kingdom of the Franks). The relevant part of the Salic Law, translated, reads as follows:

> But of Salic land no portion of the inheritance shall come to a woman: but the whole inheritance of the land shall come to the male sex.

Relevant? Surely it's pre-medieval and, in any case, has nothing to do with Britain or the English-speaking world. Yet it had an impact on British history since an extension of the Salic Law to preclude inheritance not merely by a woman but through the female line was used by the French to dispute English claims to their throne. The histories of the two countries were intertwined from the time of the Norman Conquest, and French was the official language of the court for several hundred years after 1066. The mother of Edward III, victor at the decisive battle of Crécy (1346), was the daughter of a French king and his claims on the country were based partly on family connections. When the great-grandson of Edward came to the throne in 1413 he also turned his attention to France and pursued a similar dynastic claim. In *Henry V*, Shakespeare's admiring portrait of the young and dynamic king, we see the Archbishop of Canterbury using tortuous legal language to reject the Salic Law which the French have clung to as a way of rejecting Henry's demands. The law was never meant for France, says the Archbishop, but for territory which is now part of Germany, and in any case the French kings have brushed aside the Salic Law when it suited them. All Henry requires, though, is a green light from the church to go off and fight, which he gets and does. The rest is history (Agincourt).

Three strikes (and you're out) law

The 'three strikes law' was never the official term for a penal policy that was popular in the United States in the 1990s. Instead it was referred to under such headings as the Habitual Offender Laws. The intention can be summarized as follows:

> Those convicted repeatedly of serious offences should be removed from society for long periods of time, in many cases for life.

One of several expressions from baseball which have entered the mainstream of US English, the phrase 'three strikes and you're out' describes the penalty paid by the batter after three failed attempts to hit the ball. Its metaphorical application arises from an attempt to deal with repeat criminals when many US states enacted laws requiring mandatory and extended prison sentences for those committing a third serious offence. In some states, however, the third conviction was for a relatively minor infringement. Not surprisingly, the blanket imposition of the law led to harsh penalties for a few. In California, a state which was particularly fervent in applying the 'three strikes' rule, a man with two previous robbery convictions was sentenced to twenty-five years to life for attempting to prise open the doors of a soup kitchen because he was homeless and hungry (he was released after thirteen years).The injustice of such sentencing caused the passing of Proposition 36 in California in 2012, a reform which allowed prisoners convicted under the three strikes law to petition for early release. Not only is it a humane measure but it is estimated to save California taxpayers nearly $1 billion in the next ten years.

Jim Crow Laws

This loaded expression was the name of either a song or dance associated with the plantations worked by slaves. In 1829 a white performer in Louisville, Kentucky, blackened his face to 'sing Jim Crow' and by the middle of the nineteenth century such minstrel acts had crossed the Atlantic and were to be seen in the London streets. (Unfortunately, the practice continued: the *Black and White Minstrel Show* was still playing on BBC TV in the 1970s.) After the American Civil War, many southern states enacted statutes which were intended to reinforce separation between blacks and whites, and these swiftly became known as Jim Crow Laws. They covered everything from a bar on racial intermarriage to segregation in public places such as restaurants or buses (railroad companies had separate and inferior 'Jim Crow' cars for blacks). As examples of the laws, take the following, from Alabama, Mississippi and North Carolina respectively:

No person or corporation shall require any white female nurse to nurse in wards or rooms in hospitals, either public or private, in which negro men are placed.

The marriage of a white person with a negro or mulatto or person who shall have one-eighth or more of negro blood, shall be unlawful and void.

Books shall not be interchangeable between the white and colored schools, but shall continue to be used by the race first using them.

In the twentieth century a combination of the civil rights movement, government action and rulings from the US Supreme Court slowly pushed back the Jim Crow Laws. The expression 'Jim Crow' is still in frequent use in the sense of 'bigoted' to characterize times and places in which racism was the norm. Martin Luther King remarked that Jim Crow was 'a psychological bird that told him [the white man] that no matter how bad off he was, at least he was a white man, better than the black man'.

McNaghten Rules

In 1843 Daniel M'Naghten, a Glaswegian woodturner who believed he was being persecuted by the government, fired a fatal shot at Robert Peel, the prime minister. In the event he was mistaken in his victim and it was Peel's personal secretary, Edward Drummond, who was shot in the back and died five days afterwards. At his trial M'Naghten was found not guilty by reason of insanity. In response to public unease about his acquittal, the law lords defined the grounds on which the defence of criminal insanity could be used. These became known as the M'Naghten[1] Rule(s):

> In all cases of this kind the jurors ought to be told that every man is presumed to be sane, and to possess a sufficient degree of reason to be responsible for his crimes, until the contrary

---

[1] There is disagreement over the spelling of the assassin's name. The *Oxford English Dictionary* uses McNaghten to apply to the rule while using M'Naghten for his surname. It also appears in other spellings such as McNaughton and McNaughten.

be proved to their satisfaction: and that to establish a defence on the ground of insanity, it must be clearly proved that at the time of commiting the act the party accused was labouring under such a defect of reason, from disease of the mind, as not to know the nature and quality of the act he was doing, or as not to know that what he was doing was wrong.

The 'insanity' defence is still widely upheld across the English-speaking world. Daniel M'Naghten spent his life in various asylums, dying at Broadmoor in 1865.

The Miranda Rule

In 1963 Ernesto Miranda was arrested by police in Phoenix, Arizona, on charges of kidnap and rape. He quickly confessed, was tried and convicted. But the conviction was set aside after a Supreme Court appeal, on the grounds that Miranda had not been informed by his police interrogators of a right guaranteed by the fifth amendment to the American Constitution: the right not to incriminate oneself or, in effect, the right to remain silent. Miranda was retried and found guilty on witness evidence which did not include his original confession. Yet his case was a landmark which changed the formal behaviour required of the police and which has even entered (US) English as a verb, to 'Mirandize', as in 'A police officer can "Mirandize" a criminal suspect in 10 seconds.' To be Mirandized is to be informed of one's right both to silence and to legal representation, and the procedure must take place before an interrogation, though not necessarily before an arrest. The formula is not fixed in stone but usually runs:

> You have the right to remain silent. Anything you say can and will be used against you in a court of law. You have the right to an attorney. If you cannot afford an attorney, one will be provided for you. Do you understand the rights I have just read to you? With these rights in mind, do you wish to speak to me?

The right to silence does not extend to the warning itself, since not saying anything in response to being Mirandized may indicate that the suspect does not understand or have English as a first language. In that case the Miranda must be translated and the whole process should be recorded.

After his release on parole Miranda fell back into a life of crime though his offences were less serious than the original charges or kidnap and rape. He capitalized on his legal fame by signing and selling Miranda-warning cards for $1.50. The story has an ironic end. In 1976 Ernesto Miranda, still carrying some of his autographed cards, was stabbed to death during an argument in a Phoenix skid-row bar. According to one account, the suspect was arrested but exercised his Miranda-given right to remain silent and so was released. Perhaps the police didn't bother looking too hard after that.

Index